PROVE IT OR LOSE IT

The (Mostly) No-Nonsense Guide to

Surviving Experimentation Program Drama

Rommil Santiago

EXPERIMENT NATION PUBLISHING

Prove it or Lose it
The (Mostly) No-Nonsense Guide to
Surviving Experimentation Program Drama
By Rommil Santiago

Experiment Nation Publishing
ExperimentNation.com

For Rosalie, Dahlia, Kai, and Mom: I've always loved corn.

Table of Contents

Forewords by Better Writers

Foreword by Ton Wesseling

Ton Wesseling

Experimentation Coach, Founder & Host of The Conferences known as Conversion Hotel and Experimentation Island, as well as The Experimentation Culture Awards

🌐 *tonw.com*

The importance of experimentation and evidence-based growth in the ever-evolving digital landscape cannot be overstated. As someone who has dedicated over 25 years to this industry, I have witnessed firsthand how embracing experimentation can transform organizations, unleashing their potential for innovation and sustainable growth.

With great enthusiasm, I introduce Rommil Santiago's book, "Prove It or Lose It", a no-nonsense guide to navigating the complexities of building a lasting experimentation program. It's important because, in theory, experimentation is simple; applying it lastingly in an organization is hard.

Rommil's insights are timely as they address the challenges faced by the ones running experimentation at various maturity levels in organizations.

Some organizations have integrated A/B testing into the engineering pipeline, allowing an almost effortless validation before launching new features. These organizations have also learned that well-researched hypotheses lead to successful experiments, while those lacking such rigor fall short. But, compared to every single organization being such an experimentation Valhalla, thousands of organizations are not at that maturity level.

They need a strong experimentation leader. Maybe someone like you, and perhaps you already learned that building a lasting experimentation program takes organizational savvy and proper Fingerspitzengefühl, something you must most often learn the hard way. This book is your guiding light. It delivers structure and pragmatic tips in stages, saving you from common pitfalls while building the experimentation program.

Please use the knowledge given here and help your organization grow experimentation because the greatest risk in business is not failing in an experiment but failing to experiment. Organizations can explore new avenues through experimentation, validate their ideas, and ultimately steer themselves toward success. Rommil has laid a framework that empowers you to let your organization embrace experimentation as a core principle in its strategy.

Rommil's passion for experimentation is evident throughout this book, as is his commitment to fostering a community of practitioners through Experiment Nation. His tireless efforts to connect experimenters from around the globe have not gone unnoticed; in 2021, he was honored with one of the Experimentation Culture Awards for his contributions to this field. The community he has built is a testament to his belief that collaboration and shared learning are key to advancing the practice of experimentation.

In my journey, I have been fortunate to consult for over 50 organizations across 10 countries, helping them adopt solid experimentation and validation approaches. I started agencies, developed tools, and organized events, but my love for optimization and experimentation remains unwavering. The joy of uncovering insights through testing is a driving force in my work, and this book will inspire you to experience that same joy even better.

I look forward to seeing you present your story someday on the stage of one of the events I'm organizing. But before that, I look forward to your case submission for the yearly Experimentation Culture Awards. Sharing the growth of your organization's experimentation program with the broader community and receiving praise from the international jury through a nomination, and maybe even a win, like Rommil did. Both will unlock new doors in your organization.

Happy reading!

Foreword by Khalil Guliwala

Khalil Guliwala

Marketing Manager – Client Engagement &
Growth Strategies at Creative Market
in */in/khalilguliwala/*

Humans are political animals.

From the family barbecue to the community picnic, from the prayer hall to the office, politics is a central part of human life. Yet, time and time again, those working in experimentation forget this law of human nature.

Maybe it's the pureness of experimentation that makes its practitioners believe that it is above politics. Maybe it's self-selection, with those going into experimentation being the quiet ones who believe that their work should speak for itself.

Whatever the reason, if you can't survive the politics, your best thought-out experiments, designed with mathematical precision and surgical care, end up dead on arrival.

When I talk to successful experimenters, they speak in hushed tones about how they maneuvered to get buy-in for their experiments. They want to be known for their experiments, not how they got their experiments accepted. Like how we speak about the baby, not how the baby was made.

Rommil has done something extraordinary here. Which is to take all that inside knowledge of surviving an experimentation program, till this point spoken of only in whispers, and packaged it into a book.

And you're going to come back, again and again, each time learning more about yourself and the process of getting buy-in.

Foreword by Gintarė Forshaw

Gintarė Forshaw

Co-Founder, Convertex Digital

in */in/gintare-forshaw08/*

Rommil provides a much-needed guide for those ready to elevate their experimentation programs to the next level. This is not another dry introductory text; it's an exploration of the critical elements in scaling and optimizing experimentation. Readers will find practical strategies for overcoming common bottlenecks, fostering a learning culture, and embedding experimentation into the very fabric of their organizations.

My favourite part of the book is Chapter 4, which articulates the importance of the feedback loop: continuously gathering and acting upon feedback to build the experimentation program.

Prepare to be inspired and empowered to embrace a genuinely data-driven future and build more robust experimentation programs.

Foreword by Shannon Mulligan

Shannon Mulligan

Co-Founder, *The Freelance Squad*

in */in/shannonmitchell*

Admission: I don't know a lot about experimentation.

And when I was first assigned to Rommil's experimentation pod back in 2019 at Ritual Technologies, I knew even less.

So, when Rommil asked me to write a foreword for this book, I was surprised. Was this in itself an experiment Rommil was running? Was this all just a long con to see if I could keep up the ruse?!

*But while the above is a poor attempt at a joke, there's also some truth in it. Because I **do** think it's a bit of an experiment on Rommil's part, and that's what makes him the perfect person to write a very long book about this topic.*

As a leader, a mentor, and a human being, Rommil is innately curious not just about results but about the human element that drives them. He wants to know not just the what, the why, and the how, but also the who. He cares on a deeper level about the data and choices made that mesh together to give clear and actionable next steps. It makes him not just a great experimenter but an incredible person to work with and learn from.

I'm pretty sure Rommil knew all along that I was in over my head. But instead of dismissing me as some jokey copywriter who just smiled and nodded while sweating profusely, he devoted time and energy to helping me apply experimentation to the work I was interested in.

Read this book. Tell your friends. Because if anyone can take a subject and help you discover interesting ways that it relates to your own life, it's Rommil—a brilliant and empathetic expert who cares deeply.

(Now can we talk compensation?)

This book is for experimentation program leaders (and aspiring ones)

This book is for anyone who is launching, inheriting, or managing an experimentation program but is struggling to take it to the next level. If you're finding it difficult to encourage colleagues to experiment within your organization, secure leadership support, or figure out how to position experimentation effectively for success, this guide is for you.

While I believe this book has a lot of value and oodles of advice for folks who are launching and struggling to keep their program afloat, it's important to know that this book doesn't encompass everything you need to know when starting an experimentation program from scratch.

This book doesn't provide detailed instructions on how to design experiments, specify the exact A/B testing tools you should choose, or outline which statistical approach is the best for every company. There are many resources available that cover those topics — many of which I've listed later in this book.

Getting buy-in is never a straightforward path.

What this book is, however, is a companion guide to all that other material which focuses on the challenges that are often overlooked when launching an experimentation program—especially the political ones. This book distills many of the hard-earned lessons I've gathered throughout my over 15-year career in experimentation, having repeatedly built and launched experimentation and other programs for companies across a wide range of industries and verticals.

Alongside many successes, I've also encountered my fair share of challenges. I've been dressed down in front of senior staff, I've had my program's resourcing cut, and I've even been fired. And I don't want any of those things to happen to you. That's why I, with the help of other amazingly talented (and oh so good-looking) experimentation industry veterans from the experimentation community, created this guide. I believe that the more successful experimentation programs there are in the world, the stronger the experimentation community becomes. And for me, that's something worth striving for.

Finally, it should be quite clear that this book is not particularly long (despite my rambling). I have a terrible attention span, so I don't believe a book must be long to provide value. We're all busy people — I get it. That's why you'll find summaries at the end of every chapter and a TL;DR at the end of this book.

Nothing would bring me greater satisfaction than knowing someone could read this entire book during a short flight, say from Montreal to Toronto, and walk away feeling like they've gained some useful knowledge and perspective for their experimentation practice.

So let's stop with the blah blah blah and begin.

Chapter 0
GROW to survive

The prerequisite book introduction

Let's face it — everyone loves the *idea* of experimentation. It sounds exciting, innovative, and like the perfect way to uncover hidden opportunities. But turning that dream into a reality? Not so easy. That's because running an experimentation program isn't just about running tests; it's about creating a system that delivers real, demonstrable value that **satisfies stakeholders** - and that's where most programs fall short.

Experimentation matters. A lot.

At its core, experimentation is about making better decisions. Instead of relying on gut feelings or assumptions, experimentation helps organizations use evidence to guide their choices. This reduces risk, drives efficiency (I swear), and often leads to surprising insights you wouldn't have discovered otherwise. Whether you're optimizing a marketing campaign, tweaking product features, or refining user experiences, experimentation provides the framework to validate assumptions, learn what works, and release features with confidence.

Beyond improving decisions, experimentation fosters a culture of curiosity and continuous improvement. It encourages teams to challenge assumptions, ask questions, and think creatively about solutions. Over time, this mindset helps organizations become more agile, resilient, and better equipped to adapt to changing markets or customer needs. Wow. Doesn't experimentation sound amazing?! Who wouldn't want an experimentation program right? Right?!

Your co-workers don't believe in experimentation

At *every* company I've worked at, there are always those who firmly believe that experimentation is a waste of time and slows things down. This opinion can be found everywhere from engineering to marketing to the C-suite. And it's not just at small companies, it's everywhere.

In 2019, on what was formerly known as Twitter, Ken Kocienda tweeted, "We didn't use A/B tests to make the iPhone at Apple." In 2023, Linear's Karri Saarinen said, "We don't do A/B tests. We validate ideas and assumptions that are driven by taste and opinions rather than the other way around, where tests drive decisions. There is no specific engagement or other number we look at. We beta test, see the feedback, iterate, and eventually, we have the conviction that the change or feature is as good as it can be, and we should release it to see how it works at scale."

Every company has someone who doesn't believe in experimentation.

Before you start to believe this nonsense, let me remind you that these companies have certainly had their share of major flops out in the market — but I digress. The point is, despite its benefits, **your experimentation program will always have detractors**.

A few years ago, I was working at a fast-growing SaaS

company, and the pressure was on. Senior leadership had set aggressive financial targets, and every initiative had to prove its worth. We had a new feature in the pipeline, and the team was excited—but before launching it to everyone, I pushed to run an A/B test.

That's when the debates started.

Leadership wasn't thrilled about the idea of a test. "So, you're telling me we're going to give *half* our audience a *less optimal experience?*" one executive asked, eyebrows raised. I tried to explain that *we didn't actually know which version was better yet.* The test wasn't about withholding a "superior" experience—it was about making sure we weren't about to *force a terrible one on 100% of users.*

Back and forth we went. Arguments. Counterarguments. At one point, I had over 200 comments on the same paragraphs in my test brief from every leader at the company and held a dozen meetings on the matter. I recall that one of the last things I said was, "The time it's taking us to decide on whether to run this test is more than the time it would take to actually run this test!"

In the end, reason won out. We ran the test. And sure enough, the new feature *hurt our customer's lifetime value (LTV)*. We didn't roll out the feature broadly. The test saved us from rolling out a failure to *everyone,* and the insights it generated helped shape an improved iteration. Did the company's attitude towards experimentation change afterward? I'm not sure. But I *do* know that I was invited to far more meetings about feature launches afterward.

You must constantly show value - that matters

Here's the thing. As proud as you might be about your experimentation program, **stakeholders only care about the outcomes that impact them**. Common questions you will face over the lifespan of running an experimentation program include: *Did the program drive revenue? Save costs? Improve user satisfaction? Reduce technical debt? Reduce feature rollbacks? Do you really need this much budget? Do we have to be so careful? Will it introduce site instability? Can people hack us through the experimentation tool?*

If you can't connect your efforts to not just tangible business outcomes but to the ones that your sponsors and leadership care about (especially the unspoken ones), your program will struggle to gain traction and keep funding. And worse, if you have *no outcomes* to show for all your effort yet, what then?

This is why "Prove It or Lose It" should be the mantra of any successful experimentation program leader. (Go ahead, say it to yourself a few times. I'll wait.) **By carefully crafting how you share the value of your program from the start**, you'll build trust, gain support, and hopefully enjoy continued employment.

In the following (short) chapters, we'll dive into the nuts and bolts of tackling the politics of launching and running an experimentation program. Sit tight.

The GROW framework

The GROW framework is a self-preservation tool that helps remind you to continuously communicate the value of your experimentation program throughout its various maturity stages. By structuring your actions around the pillars of this framework, you will provide a clear, concise, *and impactful* narrative that resonates with your stakeholders. What does **GROW** stand for?

Goals that resonate
Set and share goals and roadmaps that put your stakeholders' skin in the game.

Reputation matters
Build a strong, positive brand for yourself and your program.

Optimize for progress
Focus on progress over perfection to keep the momentum going.

Welcome all the feedback
Revisit and adapt because nothing stays perfect forever.

To help you remember this framework, I've created a handy-dandy graphic for you. Feel free to print this out and hang it on the wall in your office or cubicle, keep it in your wallet, or get it tattooed on your body. Wherever you decide to keep it, it's a handy reference that I use to remind myself to regularly step back from the day-to-day of running experiments and remind stakeholders of why my experimentation program is critical not only to the business but to them as well.

The following chapters dive into each pillar in detail.

The GROW Framework

Goals that resonate
Set and share goals and roadmaps that put your stakeholders' skin in the game.

Reputation matters
Build a strong, positive brand for yourself and your program.

Optimize for progress
Focus on progress over perfection to keep the momentum going.

Welcome all the feedback
Revisit and adapt because nothing stays perfect forever.

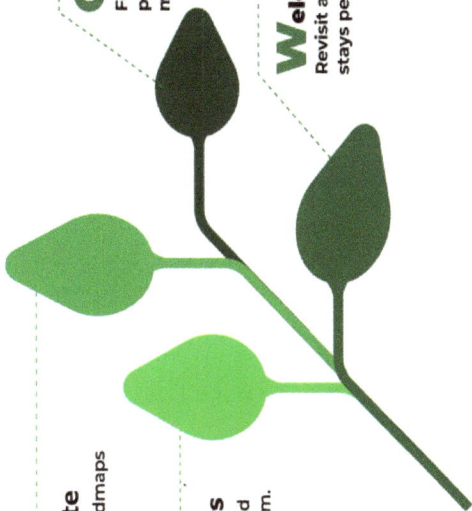

EXPERIMENT NATION

Chapter 1
Goals that resonate

The experimentation culture trifecta

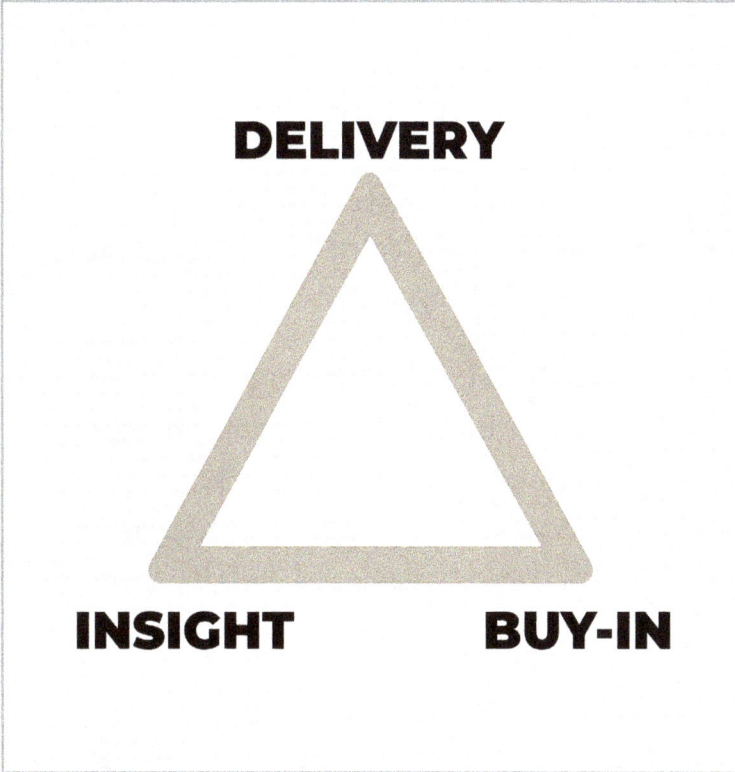

The experimentation culture trifecta

A healthy experimentation culture comes down to three key ingredients:

1. **Delivery** - The ability to deliver different experiences to your audience
2. **Insight** - The ability to analyze and trust the test results
3. **Buy-in** - The support from leaders and key stakeholders that matter

Modern experimentation tools usually take care of the first two, or you can bring in talent to fill the gaps. But that third one—getting buy-in—is the tricky part.

A lot of effort goes into getting approval for the tools, but not nearly enough to maintain support for growing the experimentation program. Without buy-in, your experimentation culture will fail to flourish and is doomed to failure. Unfortunately, getting buy-in is the tricky bit.

Me, me, me

"I've always believed that if you put in the work, the results will come."

– Michael Jordan

"You are not the main character in anyone else's story."

– Halsey

Most stakeholders don't like risks or unknowns when it comes to things that impact their work and goals. Despite an experimentation program's reliance on processes, data, and uncovering the unknown, **experimentation results are inherently unpredictable and uncertain**. The only certainty is that experiments will cost money and take time away from something else (even if they help generate revenue and avert loss).

That's why when a company takes the leap and decides to adopt an experimentation program, stakeholders will inevitably ask two questions (in various forms):

1. *What will it deliver?*
2. *How will it be delivered?*

However, what they really mean to ask is:

1. *What will it deliver* me?
2. *How will delivering that* impact me?

While your company's experimentation maturity (i.e. its skill level in running and learning from tests) plays a role in how nuanced these questions are, the **answers lie in your program's goals and roadmaps**. While it's easy to pull goals out of thin air by setting arbitrary lift targets or revenue projections, a more *powerful* approach is to choose goals that key stakeholders are willing to invest in (i.e, goals for which they have **skin in the game**) and define a well-thought-out plan that **mirrors and supports their roadmaps**.

Put their skin in your game

When setting goals for an experimentation program, the flow often goes something like this (tell me if this feels familiar):

- Say you will run X experiments in a year
- Commit to achieving a lift of Y%
- Promise that the program will pay for itself in a certain period of time
- Mention how FAANG companies successfully leverage experimentation
- Finish up with an inspirational poster

It's not a bad approach. It lays out some facts, ties the program to the organization's revenue goals, and proves you can do some basic math. It's the equivalent of saying, "Hey, these aren't wild ideas I cooked up over coffee." But here's the catch: that's rarely enough to get people to *support* you.

When pitching to a room full of decision-makers, it's rare to see everyone nodding in agreement from start to finish. More likely, a few people will be distracted, perhaps sending Slack messages during your presentation, and at least one person will challenge you with tough, unexpected questions out of genuine curiosity or a desire to appear smart (or sometimes the latter framed as the former). And as you calmly respond to each question on the fly, part of you screams inside, *"Were you not listening? How are you not on board yet? Why are you asking me this? That doesn't make any sense!"*

People care about their goals - not yours.

The disconnect often stems from a failure to relate to your stakeholders' perspectives — or get *their* skin in *your* game. In the case of an experimentation program, stakeholders may not care about your goals of learning or increased revenue. Instead, they might be concerned about risks like unstable code, flickering user experiences, throwaway work, or an added burden on the analytics teams. By ignoring these concerns upfront, **you undermine your credibility** and risk your program's success.

The $100M Testing Culture Shift

A few years ago, while leading experimentation at a large retailer, I couldn't understand why product teams weren't experimenting often or why they seemed indifferent to the results when they did. Despite the value experimentation could bring, it seemed like they considered it a distraction from "real work."

Eventually, I realized the core issue: nearly all product managers were measured on their ability to launch and deliver features, not on the impact those features had. Their success was defined by shipping what they had committed to, not by whether those features actually improved performance.

I know what you're thinking: Why wouldn't a product organization care if its features worked? Believe me, these were highly skilled product managers - they cared. Unfortunately, the company allocated resources based on the promise of shiny new features they could showcase to their shareholders and board of directors. In fact, very little attention was paid to proving the performance of those features - until the company started falling short of its revenue goals, of course.

So, it was no surprise to me that product management was in a panic every fourth quarter. Because they hadn't run experiments throughout the year, teams scrambled to figure out whether their work had made *any* meaningful difference - and without control groups, you can imagine how fun that was. By the end of every year, leadership criticized the product team for not delivering real value and missing revenue goals. Rinse and repeat.

After a year or so of this nonsense, I reframed the experimentation program's purpose—not just to drive revenue but to prevent losses. If the product team couldn't always demonstrate that their features generated revenue, we could at least show that their experiments helped avoid costly missteps. By the following year, the product team had quadrupled the number of tests it ran and demonstrated over $100 million in combined revenue gains and cost savings. It was a number no one could ignore.

At another company, I led a growth program across multiple divisions and countries, but the teams saw testing as just another box to tick - something they had to do rather than something they wanted to do.

To change that, I met with each team to understand what truly mattered to them. One team was focused on generating traffic, another on acquiring new customers, and a third on P&L. Meanwhile, the testing program wasn't directly tied to any of these goals, making it easy for teams to disengage.

So, I restructured the program to align with their priorities and position it as an enabler of their success. Once I made it so that their key metrics were reflected in my program's objectives, everything changed. With this alignment, engagement skyrocketed. Teams proactively mentioned how they ran tests to achieve their goals and were always coming up with new things to investigate. And probably most importantly, it became a lot easier to demonstrate the program's impact—both on individual teams and on the business as a whole.

The CEO at one of my previous jobs often said, *"Everyone makes sense in their head."* That has stuck with me for years. It's a simple yet profound truth, and I've shared it with every mentee I've had ever since. What it means is that people's decisions and actions always align with **their** beliefs and interests. In business, while you and your stakeholders generally share overarching goals, disagreements usually stem from folks **having their skin in different games**.

For example, an engineer may fully support revenue growth but will prioritize keeping a website stable because that is the goal they are accountable for, or perhaps maintaining a stable site is a point of pride for them. A designer might welcome customer insights but won't be thrilled about creating countless assets to support personalization. A product leader may see an experimentation program risking their timelines rather than delivering value. The point is that your stakeholders will care less about your goals and more about how your program affects them achieving theirs (official or otherwise).

So, how do you get stakeholders to care and support you?
Here are a few strategies:

Identify who doesn't matter, and focus on those who do

Influence doesn't always follow the organizational chart.

The first order of business is to figure out who you *don't* need to get buy-in from. Get clarity on each stakeholder's role and decision-making power. Start by looking up your company's org chart, asking peers, and setting up introductory coffee chats. As you learn more about the power dynamics at your company, you'll start to understand who wields actual influence and who doesn't. Don't let fancy titles fool you. You'd be surprised how often folks ignore the person with the highest title.

Among those who have actual influence, decide which of them you truly need support from. For example, you may not need the backing of customer support for launching an experimentation program, but you will surely need that from finance. Remember, just like in life, you can't please them all — focus less on pleasing those who don't matter to your program and more on those who do.

Next, understand their responsibilities and identify what they are most invested in. Understand their official and unofficial KPIs. Suppose a stakeholder is constantly concerned with revenue, customer satisfaction, or operational efficiency. In that case, tailoring your communications to how your experimentation program supports their *official KPIs* will help set them up as a future ally. But don't stop there. It's not just about *what* you say but *how* you say it.

Look at emails, reports, meeting notes, and other documents highlighting these stakeholders' *personal* preferences or *personality quirks* (bonus points if you leverage AI). This will give you a sense of how they like to be treated and how they measure their personal success (aka their *unofficial KPIs*), which will help you land your message better.

Years ago, I used to work with a product manager who would always lose his temper when he didn't feel he was given the respect he deserved. If a decision was made without him, he would be intolerable - even if the decision made was the right one. If he felt we were wasting his time, he was obnoxious - even if the matter was important. This behaviour came through the way he spoke, sent messages, *everything*. It was clear that one of his unofficial KPIs was to be treated like a god.

Usually I would just ignore assholes like him. But I needed his support for a program I was growing. So, I decided to lean into his unofficial KPI by greeting him every morning with a joking salute and saying, "Good morning, Lord of Sea and Sky!" After a few days of this, he started to treat me differently and became more open to my ideas. He began to salute back and eventually bounce ideas off of me. In turn, I bounced ideas off of him related to my program.

Was this a form of manipulation? Perhaps. Did it get the job done? Absolutely. Now, I'm not saying that everyone needs to pander to the office asshole. But what I am saying is this: you can get even the crankiest adversary on your side if you understand what they value officially and unofficially. Maybe they like to talk about their weekend, a hobby, or their kids. You'll find folks tend to light up when talking about things they love. If you become the source of a little joy in their day, that is something you can leverage by starting your conversations with one of those topics. At best, you earn their trust. At worst, get it wrong and uncover some hot-button topics to steer clear of.

Persuade constructively

Constructive persuasion is a key skill for advancing and growing your experimentation program. It helps you secure buy-in, push ideas forward, and, most importantly, eliminate unnecessary barriers that could slow you down. While it can sometimes feel uncomfortable, **navigating messy politics is an essential skill** for any experimentation leader. But what if politics are not your strong suit? Or if you aren't quick on your feet during large meetings? The following are some tactics you should consider.

Pre-Suade, pre-suade, pre-suade

Schedule informal (or formal if you are feeling fancy) meetings to **ask important stakeholders directly** about what matters to them and their opinion of your experimentation program. These smaller meetings make it easier for them to open up and speak freely. Doing this also shows that you care about what they think, gives you direct insight into some of the nuances of their world and hopefully gives you a chance to persuade (aka pre-suade) them on contentious topics before larger meetings. Addressing their concerns in a private forum prevents negative sentiments from influencing others. Finally, if you succeed in gaining an ally, it's always nice to have a supporter in the room while you present ideas.

Ask for their expertise

If leading meetings like that isn't really your style, try asking for advice from someone whose support you need instead. Asking someone for advice is a great way to turn them into an ally. First off, it shows that you respect their opinion and trust their experience - making them feel good and more positively about you. Everyone likes to feel helpful; when you ask for advice, you give them that chance.

It also creates a small sense of partnership. Once someone gives you advice, they often feel more connected to your journey and might even root for you to succeed. This taps into something called the *Benjamin Franklin Effect*, where doing someone a favor (like giving advice) makes us like them more.

Finally, asking for advice opens the door to keep the *conversation going*. You can follow up, share progress, and build a real relationship over time. So, while it might feel like a small ask, reaching out for advice can be a low-key way to build trust, create goodwill, and get someone on your side.

Practice dark arts sparingly

I only recommend the following tactics if you had no luck with any of the previously listed approaches because, honestly, they're kind of creepy. But sometimes you gotta do what you gotta do.

Grab their attention by mentioning their interest

Consider reviewing stakeholders' social media profiles (e.g. LinkedIn, their portfolio websites, etc.) to understand their interests, priorities, and recent achievements. Pay attention to the content they share, comment on, like, as well as the tone they use, as these can reveal some shared interests that you can leverage. For example, maybe they have a hobby you can mention in an example. (Mentions of volleyball and photography always work on me.)

Rub elbows with their online groups

Participate in LinkedIn groups, forums, or Twitter discussions where your stakeholders are active. These groups often focus on topics that matter to them, such as market trends, business challenges, or new technologies. Engaging in these spaces can provide deeper insights into the challenges and goals that are top of mind for stakeholders. At minimum, you may appear in their feed, and they may feel more acquainted with you.

Considerations when inheriting an existing program

In the case you are asked to take over an existing experimentation program, even if you have access to top-notch A/B testing tools, a skilled team, and endless enthusiasm, keeping a program running—or, even better, evolving—requires persistence, strategic thinking, and, most importantly, a clear understanding of **why the program was started in the first place**. This clarity is vital information to help you decide what goals to set and what plans to develop to garner more support.

The program could have started for any number of reasons – perhaps there was an urgent need to generate more revenue from the company's website, or it stemmed from a top-down directive after your CEO read an HBR article. It might have been initiated by the product management team, who believed that product managers needed stronger

Sometimes, we inherit ill-fitting things.

skills to critically evaluate their work and assumptions.
Whatever the case, here's the tricky part — your manager
or other stakeholders may not openly share the true reason
the program was approved. It could be that you aren't able
to reach any former employees involved with the program.
Or perhaps the program was green-lit by a senior leader
who had their own set of expectations about what the

program should deliver but has since left the company. To make things more complicated, it's also typical for the program's purpose to shift over time due to changing organizational priorities or political dynamics. Sometimes, it is just easier to reboot the program entirely, realigning its goals and operations to fit the new pressures or expectations that have emerged. But when you don't have that kind of luxury, let's look at some common management behaviours and what they tell you about why your program (still) exists.

What management says or does	Why the program exists
Never asks for test evidence while making decisions.	To prove leadership's decisions were the right ones.
Focuses on test velocity.	To demonstrate that the company is cutting-edge.
Asks for a win rate forecast.	To generate predictable revenue.
Ignores you.	The program was an executive's idea – but they've left the company.
Gives you no resources.	To be autonomous and fix all the problems.
They ask analysts to dig into test results from multiple angles over and over.	To prove leadership's decisions were the right ones.
Experimentation does not have any OKRs.	No one remembers, but other functions are more important.
Asks for results immediately.	Generate revenue – probably to save the company from ruin.
Ignores test results in favour of opinion.	To prove leadership's decisions were the right ones.
Asks you to present experimentation to countless groups repeatedly.	To be a change agent.
To partner with teams to co-develop testing roadmaps.	To level up staff.

Seek context if things go sideways

That said, despite best efforts, even after countless rounds of negotiations about goals and plans with stakeholders, they often don't land the way we want — and conversations start to go sideways. If you find yourself in this situation, stop what you're doing and make it a priority to gather more context immediately. Don't hesitate to ask, "Can you help me understand why you disagree?" or "I sense some doubt about this proposal, can you help me understand your hesitation?"

I know this can feel intimidating at first—it takes practice and courage because we often fear appearing uninformed or not in agreement with others. But I urge you to fight that impulse and ask for clarity. Instead of coming across as unsure, you'll position yourself as a true partner, someone committed to understanding their perspective. It's your responsibility to bridge the gap and ensure that everyone aligns on what success looks like for your program.

Set eyes on the right prizes

"What gets measured gets managed."

— Peter Drucker

When nurturing a culture of experimentation, tracking the right things reinforces the right behaviours and attracts more stakeholder support. You might be saying to yourself, *"OK, that's all well and good, but can you just tell me about some metrics I should consider?!"*

Example goals

Here are some examples of KPIs to consider incorporating into your experimentation program to increase the chances that your stakeholders support you. I strongly suggest you tweak these to make them more relevant to your stakeholders, work environment, etc.

Engineering goals

- Percentage of experiments implemented without causing downtime or major bugs.
- Time taken to roll back an experiment in case of failure.

- Impact on platform performance/load time.
- Reduction in experiment implementation time (cycle time for coding experiments).

Finance goals

- Incremental revenue generated per experiment on average.
- Total revenue lift achieved by experiments within a fiscal quarter.
- Average cost per experiment (or a proxy).
- Percentage of experiments achieving positive ROI within a set timeframe.
- Losses averted.

Design goals

- Percentage of experiments showing improvements in key usability metrics (e.g., task completion time, CES, etc.).
- The number of experiments designed to test accessibility improvements.

Efficiency goals

- Time spent on creating design assets for experiments as a percentage of total project time.

Survival techniques for each experimentation maturity phase

In addition to adapting to the needs of your stakeholders, you must evolve your ways of working as your program. Every experimentation program matures through three phases, and the experimentation program leader should take specific actions throughout each. Those phases are:

1. Kickoff: Building leadership's confidence.
2. Establishing ways of working.
3. Expanding a culture of experimentation across the organization.

It might be tempting to be proactive and try to tackle every stage at once, but that'll just stretch you, your focus, and your resources too thin. Let's go through each stage one by one and go over the things you should do for each.

Kickoff: Building leadership's confidence

The kickoff phase centers on building and keeping leadership's trust by demonstrating that the experimentation program can deliver the value that they expected. Your primary focus should be on producing visible results—whether through quick wins or interesting (if not strategic) insights. So, make sure you do most of the following:

- **Update frequently** - Leadership wants to see steady, focused progress on tool implementation and/or your first test(s). One example of something you could report on is the percentage of completion for the implementation.

- **Deliver an outcome no matter how small** - Show that testing can deliver measurable benefits, even on a small scale, to demonstrate your program will be ROI-positive. A metric you could report on is the annualized impact of a test if the company were to scale it to your entire audience. Sometimes, you can avoid the ROI conversations during the early stages of your program as you lay the foundation for your program - but I don't recommend it. Your program is at its highest risk until you can show tangible returns.

- **Avoid blame as much as possible -** First impressions count. *I promise you* that everyone will blame your experimentation program for everything from missing financial targets to site instability to organizational chaos. If issues arise that could potentially point the blame towards your program, quickly perform a root cause analysis to clear your program's reputation immediately. If the issue ends up being the fault of your experimentation program, own up quickly and recommend some actions to remedy the situation immediately. If you fail to do so, you'll find yourself at the heart of every issue, and blame will be something that will dog your program forever. Everyone loves a scapegoat. Consider reporting on Tool Uptime to demonstrate that your experimentation tool wasn't down as often as some may have thought.

- **Welcome ideas, just not all of them -** Be open to accepting ideas from across the organization.

However, you must manage submissions carefully to avoid overwhelming the experimentation team and disappointing contributors whose ideas don't gain traction. Consider reporting on the number of ideas submitted and/or the number of those that lead to experiments.

- **Avoid overestimating but never underestimate impact** - Inevitably, you will be asked to estimate the impact of a test or your program. You will not be able to avoid it forever. Know that finance will constantly be looking for places to cut costs, and experimentation is always on the short list. Unfortunately, estimating the impact of an experimentation program can be tricky. You'll often need a global holdout and/or factor in diminishing returns of a change, seasonality, market trends, etc.

One technique that I've always found useful for forecasts is called annualization. **Annualization** is a way to take the lift of a test (or the average lift of a series of tests) and project it over a full year. It helps you demonstrate the magnitude of a change without committing to a figure. For example, if your program saved $5,000 in one month, your annualized loss averted would be $60,000 ($5,000 x 12). Remember to adjust your estimate to reflect the savings as if the change were exposed to your entire audience.

Another approach to consider is pro forma. **Pro forma** is a fancy way of saying "what if". For instance, if we were to see an X% lift in Add to Carts from a test, we can expect to see $Y in revenue. This way, you don't commit to delivering a dollar value, but you are also giving them an idea of the magnitude of a test. In both of these, you avoid underestimating the impact of your work — which, at this stage, is very important.

- **Build a trophy case** - Keep a well-organized, easily accessible repository of test wins. At some point, a leader will ask for key learnings or proof that your program has been worth the investment, and you don't want to waste a day scrambling to put it together—have it ready at all times. As you build your "trophy case" of wins, you'll start to be recognized as the go-to expert and a driver of growth. Use this to your advantage—you'll need it when times get tough. And trust me, those moments will come. With this in mind, it's often beneficial to report on your win rate or the percentage of tests that result in a positive result. Just be careful, though. You don't want leadership to be too focused on win rate, learning is important too.

Establishing ways of working

Once your team has completed a few successful tests, the next phase involves creating and sharing **standardized processes** to bring order and predictability to your program. While you'll have a rough idea of what makes a good flow for your organization during your initial tests, during this stage, you will want to begin refining how experimentation integrates into broader workflows. I prefer less rigid processes — ones that can flex with demands - but each organization has its preferences. For example, some companies need a fairly complex workflow to accommodate their politics. At other companies, lightweight processes help accommodate frequent reorganizations. However it plays out, the key objectives of this stage are:

- **Reducing thrash** - Chaos can be very unsettling for many. Keeping things orderly, documented, and predictable alleviates much stakeholder tension.

- **Improving efficiency** - Streamline the path from idea to execution. Consider reporting on the time to production and highlight any bottlenecks.

- **Impacting strategy** - Ensure that test results inform meaningful changes and decisions. You may want to keep track and report on the number of strategic decisions impacted by each test.

Spreading a culture of experimentation across the organization

During this phase, your program evolves into a company-wide initiative. The focus shifts to fostering a culture of experimentation, where teams across the organization can contribute ideas, learn from tests, and even run their own experiments. The success of an experimentation program during this phase is often measured by its ability to:

- **Achieve scale** - Broaden the range of business areas and metrics addressed by experiments. A nice way to illustrate this is to report test activity broken out by functional area.

- **Increase participation** - Act on ideas from various teams to foster engagement and inclusivity. Reporting on the percentage of certain teams involved in experimentation is helpful here.

- **Enable self-service** - Empower others to run tests independently while maintaining program integrity. You can leverage documentation views or A/B testing platform logins here.

Watch out for gaming

Keep an eye out for people gaming your program's metrics, intentionally or not. Gaming the system can compromise the program's credibility as a decision-making methodology.

Gaming is when an individual within the company takes actions that improve metrics but in a way that doesn't contribute to the business. Examples include increasing test velocity with A/A tests or tests with very weak hypotheses and low likelihood impact, similar to how some athletes pad their stats but don't help their team win.

I've seen this happen time and time again, but there's one instance that really stands out. A marketing team I once worked with was assigned to generate leads for a product line and would proudly report impressive numbers week after week. But one day, a co-worker and I came across a budget spreadsheet—and reality hit. It turned out they were spending hundreds of dollars per lead only to bring in customers with a lifetime value of just $50 to $100.

Knowing that our budget was tight, we asked them how they could justify knowingly losing the company money.

Their response? "My goal is to generate leads. No one said they had to be profitable."

Getting ahead of gaming requires proactive measures to realign incentives and promote genuine learning. Here are some ways to tackle this issue:

- **Shift the focus to quality metrics** - Redefine success by also tracking metrics that emphasize the value of experiments rather than their quantity or win rate. For example, measure the number of actionable insights generated, the percentage of key business areas tested, or how experiments influenced broader decision-making. Celebrate experiments that deliver important learnings, even if they don't result in a win. This change in focus encourages teams to design thoughtful, impactful tests instead of superficial ones aimed at padding numbers. Note that you may be tempted to do this out of the gate, but in most cases, I recommend that you don't, as it may hinder teams from building momentum.

- **Introduce an approval process** - Implement a system where proposed experiments undergo approval before being allowed to run. This can involve other experimenters or program leaders evaluating test hypotheses, design, and alignment with strategic goals. This also ensures that experiments are well thought through and creates accountability by reducing the temptation to launch low-quality tests only to meet targets. Additionally, it fosters collaboration and knowledge-sharing, strengthening the overall program. The only problem with this approach is that it is hard to get on people's busy schedules — so grab that time well in advance.

- **Share results publicly** - Regularly share the outcomes of experiments—both wins and losses—with a wide audience. Highlight what was learned, even from unsuccessful tests, and tie those learnings back to business goals. This transparency shifts the narrative from "only wins matter" to "every experiment contributes to growth and understanding." Publicly recognizing teams that share meaningful insights, regardless of success, reinforces a culture of genuine experimentation and discourages gaming behaviours.

Present digestible roadmaps

While program goals demonstrate your commitment to helping your company and your stakeholders achieve success through experimentation, roadmaps demonstrate your competence and preparedness to bring those goals to life.

However, like every other program, experimentation programs never have enough resources. If you work on a centralized experimentation team, you probably have a huge backlog of tests to get through. If you're part of an embedded team, chances are you're not getting as much engineering help as you'd like. And no matter how you are structured, you're probably short on analytics support. When so much of your success depends on other teams, it can be tough to put together a testing plan or learning roadmap that not only gets the support you need but is doable.

Here are a few approaches to developing experimentation roadmaps that have worked for me.

Group test ideas into themes and prioritize them

Being organized often improves others' opinion of you because it demonstrates that you have a clear thought process and can communicate ideas effectively. When you're on top of things, you come across as efficient, reliable, and good at solving problems - traits people associate with experimentation leaders. So it is in your best interest to organize your test ideas into themes and, by using all the data at your disposal, prioritize them in terms of potential impact on the business. Your roadmap should reflect these themes and prioritization to avoid your program from being labelled as random or (gasp) not strategic enough.

Have a plan B for when you miss targets

If there's one universal truth in CRO, it's this: no matter what goals you have, be prepared to fall short. Not because you're bad at your job, not because you didn't work hard enough, but because that's just the nature of the game. CRO takes serious mental toughness to keep showing up, test after test, knowing that even your best work might not hit the lofty targets set for you. Know that leadership sets

Some targets are easier to hit than others.

aggressive goals for a reason. They're pushing for maximum impact, and that means stretching the limits of what's possible.

It can be frustrating and sometimes demoralizing, but it's also part of the job. Accepting that it is normal to fall short is a survival skill in this field. My trick to surviving (at least politically) the times when your program falls short is showcasing that you have backup plans. Sharing alternate paths of exploration should a particular focus not pan out inspires confidence that you've been there and done that. Throughout the year, keep generating new ideas, new insights, and new angles so that you are always one or even two steps ahead.

And when you *do* hit those goals? Celebrate, of course! Enjoy the win because they don't come easy. Just don't get too comfortable—leadership will probably double those targets the second you crack them. Unfortunately, the reward for good work is more work. With that said, don't take it personally; it's just how business works. They're chasing growth, and your success is proof there's more potential left to tap.

Work ahead of others

Reserving a part of your A/B testing roadmap to test assumptions and opportunities ahead of product management or marketing work is a smart move because not only does it help inform and de-risk their work, but it also minimizes the chances of your tests overlapping with the launch of new features or messaging in the same areas.

By validating other teams' key hypotheses early, they can get an early read on what resonates with customers, refine their strategies, and avoid costly missteps. This proactive approach fosters a partnership mindset and encourages evidence-driven decision-making. The main challenge with this approach is that you need to be on top of other teams' best ideas, which will change often. To address this, I strongly recommend regular touchpoints (via Slack if scheduling is hard or via Microsoft Teams if you dislike yourself) with these teams to ensure you are in the loop and to negotiate getting some engineering support for your tests.

As I mentioned, being a scouting party can also prevent your tests from overlapping with others' work. As someone who has had many meetings about finding ways that experimentation or growth can operate without interfering with product development or marketing campaigns, let me tell you, it's the kind of meeting you want to avoid, as they can hurt your credibility.

Work on the same things as others

An alternative to exploring opportunities ahead of others' work is to work in *lockstep* with them. In other words, only test things that other teams are currently working on. This reduces duplication of effort and ensures testing resources are focused where they can have the greatest impact. Integrating testing into the others' roadmaps better highlights experimentation's value as a decision-making tool because more eyes will be on the program's work. The main gotcha here is that you'll need to embed yourself with many teams, which makes it hard to keep track of things. But if you're able to demonstrate success by being embedded with a couple of teams, you may be able to build a case for more experimentation resources.

Be the SWAT team

Creating an A/B testing roadmap that focuses on uncovering and addressing broader conversion rate issues or misunderstood areas *independently* allows you to generate valuable learnings and revenue without depending on other teams. This self-sufficient, proactive approach not only boosts revenue but also enhances the testing team's reputation as a critical driver of innovation and growth. Everyone loves a hero.

While appealing, this approach has potential downsides. It might foster a siloed mindset, where testing efforts focus on short-term gains at the expense of aligning with long-term strategic goals, potentially causing friction with other teams, such as product or marketing. Additionally, concentrating solely on problem areas can lead to a reactive, fire-fighting approach that addresses symptoms rather than tackling root causes or exploring opportunities for innovation. There's also the risk of diminishing returns, as repeatedly addressing issues in isolation will eventually yield fewer wins over time. To ensure these efforts remain impactful, it's often best to regularly share your priorities with and seek regular input from senior leadership and peers.

Prepare for pushback

Whichever approach you take to craft your roadmap, depending on your stakeholders, you can expect pushback from at least one of a few angles, such as:

- **Fear or slowdown** - Stakeholders might worry that testing will slow down their timelines, delaying the launch of new features or campaigns.

- **Concern about resource constraints** - Teams could argue they lack the bandwidth, budget, or engineering support to conduct tests, especially if they perceive the testing process as an added burden.

- **Territorial egos** - Product, marketing, or design leaders may feel their experience and insights are sufficient, questioning the need to validate assumptions through testing.

- **Skepticism of the importance of experimentation** - There may be doubts about whether the insights from testing will be actionable or relevant enough to justify the effort.

If you find yourself in this situation, here are a few things to highlight to hopefully ease some of these concerns:

- **Experimentation reduces rework** - Emphasize how early testing reduces the risk of rework or failed initiatives later, ultimately saving time. Emphasize the political headaches you can avoid in the case you have to roll back a mistake. Also, highlight how testing can run in parallel with other workstreams to minimize delays.

- **It can be lean** - Present a lean testing approach that requires minimal resources, such as quick-and-dirty fake door experiments or leveraging existing tools and data. Emphasize that low-fi tests can generate as much insight as high-fidelity ones.

- **It validates and quantifies beliefs** - Frame testing as a way to validate intuition rather than replace it. Don't underestimate the political opportunity around generating experimental evidence that supports a stakeholder's opinion. You'll often find that people's opinions of experimentation change when it proves them right.

- **It's like QA but more informative** - Frame testing as a natural part of execution in the same ways that QA and research are. Highlight how your competitors leverage experimentation. Don't underestimate the power of keeping up with the Joneses.

Advice from CRO experts

Using goal trees

Sam Barber

Senior Experimentation Specialist
at Suncorp Bank
🔗 */in/sam-barber-bb403a55/*

Hosting a goal tree mapping workshop with stakeholders or a stand-alone session based on your understanding is a great way to both build relationships and demonstrate how your program's strategies link directly back to stakeholder and business goals.

Getting goals on a whiteboard or Miro board provides you with a great visual record of what stakeholders are trying to achieve and provides them with a tangible link to how all of your initiatives drive them toward their goals.

The outputs are also a great reference for the wider business on the benefits of experimentation linking back to the overall strategy.

The power of loss averted

Lucas Vos

Senior Conversion Specialist at RTL

in */in/lucasfjvos/*

Every CRO sometimes has the hard job of presenting the outcome of an experiment that showed opposite results than expected. Especially when management has high expectations, it can be something very scary, as you might feel you'll be that messenger who will be shot when bringing the message.

When we reframed the experiments with negative outcomes as 'loss averted' instead of 'loser' or similar, we faced a lot less pushback while presenting sometimes painful outcomes. We just presented it as 'Glad we have tested it; otherwise, we would have lost far more money, ' which proved to be a very digestible message for senior management. I would definitely recommend other CROs/experimenters to frame it like that as well.

Getting buy-in

Ana Catarina Cizilio

Experimenter and Conversion Optimizer for 10 years

 /in/anacizilio/

When we think of buy-in for experimentation, we often think about leadership or stakeholders. But don't forget about people who can make experiments happen: designers, developers, analysts, SEO, and more. Having buy-in and excitement from those players will also make your experimentation program well-accepted and successful. Ego and politics are the most difficult parts to deal with in any company — it's very common to have a great idea or result ignored because someone 'didn't like it' or felt left out. Play along, merge roadmaps and goals, and run some surveys – you can be surprised by how many good ideas and results can come from other teammates.

Being an impactful experimentation program manager

Will Feng

*Principal Conversion
Optimization Lead*
in /in/willfeng

Experimentation inherently requires strong analytical skills—your ability to interpret data, draw insights, and make data-driven decisions is essential. However, being purely analytical is not enough. To truly excel, you must broaden your expertise across multiple disciplines, such as engineering, design, QA, finance, leadership, marketing, and product management. Having a working knowledge of these areas allows you to:

1. *Better engage with stakeholders.*
2. *Understand the challenges teams face.*
3. *Identify opportunities to optimize the experimentation workflow.*
4. *Steer your organization toward impactful, data-informed improvements.*

Below are a few areas where deeper knowledge can enhance your effectiveness, along with some examples of how they tie into experimentation.

Engineering

- ***Increasing development velocity***
  If you work with developers, share tool-specific knowledge through documentation, internal wikis, or informal lunch-and-learns. This helps new team members onboard quicker, reducing downtime and accelerating test development.

- ***Optimizing experiment performance***
  If you're using a client-side experimentation tool, consider placing the JavaScript snippet in a way that minimizes page load delays—such as asynchronously or closer to the site's header. Alternatively, invest in a server-side solution to reduce client-side dependencies and improve overall site performance.

Design

- ***Adhering to brand guidelines***
  Your wireframe might look great in theory, but if it doesn't follow existing design systems or brand standards, it could be scrapped. Partner with designers early to incorporate the right fonts, colour schemes, and component libraries.

- ***Bridging the gaps***
  Some details (e.g., hover states, responsive layouts, or micro-interactions) are often omitted from wireframes, leaving developers to guess. Document these elements upfront to reduce rework and improve consistency.

Leadership and management

- ***Tailoring experiment results***
  When presenting to leadership, avoid overwhelming them with granular testing details. Instead, highlight key insights and overall impact and tie results to higher-level KPIs / strategic goals.

- ***Aligning metrics and goals***
  If your wins don't align with leadership's metrics, revisit your success criteria to ensure they influence their KPIs.

As an experimentation program manager, think of yourself as the "mini-CEO" of your program. You'll touch nearly every department, which means you can't limit yourself to a narrow role. Your versatility and willingness to learn across multiple domains will set you apart as an orchestrator of cross-functional success.

And remember, in an era where AI tools are increasingly accessible, it can be your partner in making technical concepts more approachable. Whether you need to dissect complex data pipelines or generate new test ideas, leverage AI as a consultative ally to keep your experimentation program running at the cutting edge.

Chapter 1 summary

- Successful experimentation isn't just about running tests—it's about making stakeholders care and see its value.

- Most stakeholders are risk-averse and care more about how an experimentation program will impact their goals than anything else.

- To get buy-in, align your program's objectives with stakeholders' priorities and concerns. Instead of setting success metrics in a silo, involve stakeholders so they have "skin in the game."

- Connect with key decision-makers (and ignore those that don't matter) to understand their official and unofficial KPIs and frame experimentation as a tool for avoiding losses, not just driving revenue.

- Consider asking for advice to leverage the Benjamin Franklin Effect.

- Preempt pushback and highlight wins strategically.

Chapter 2
Reputation matters

The importance of a positive brand

As one can assume, building a positive brand for yourself in the early days of your program greatly influences how colleagues, managers, and stakeholders perceive it. Having a strong positive brand helps you navigate company dynamics and push through challenges as you transition between experimentation maturity phases. The building blocks of a strong brand (at least when it comes to leading an experimentation program) are:

Being seen as:

- Likeable
- An agent of change
- An expert leader
- Experienced
- A winner
- In control of your program's messaging

Let's explore each one in turn and make you a star.

The power of likeability

The problem with many experimenters and conversion rate optimizers is that while they are logical, they often ignore the importance of being likeable. Admit it. You know what I'm talking about - the kinds of people who don't seem to understand how awful they come across as they belittle others for not doing things the way they prefer to.

When working with other teams, **being right is not enough**. Even the most well-crafted A/B testing roadmaps will fall flat if people don't like the person behind them. Think about it - how often do you jump at the chance to collaborate with someone you constantly clash with? Do you go to bat for someone who always makes you feel inferior? Being likeable might not be what everyone talks about, but it's a game-changer - especially when you're trying to launch an experimentation program.

Being perceived as approachable and easy to work with increases the chances that others will **listen to your ideas and back your plans**. People naturally support those they enjoy working with.

People want to work with people they like.

When people feel good about working with you, they're also **more likely to open up** - whether it's to share concerns, offer feedback, or brainstorm ideas. That openness to share honest feedback helps you **spot**

potential problems early and adapt your plans before they escalate into bigger issues.

The walk that humbled me

This reminds me of a time when I was leading eCommerce for a particular territory; I often found myself clashing with a peer from another region. I was constantly pushing for new initiatives backed by market trends and data, but my approach seemed to rub them the wrong way every time. The tension was clear, but I didn't fully understand why—until a business trip changed everything.

One evening, we took the time to grab a drink and go for a long walk. Our conversation naturally drifted beyond work—we talked about our childhoods, our career paths, and events that shaped us. We discovered that we had a shared perspective on many things in life. It was an organic, eye-opening exchange.

I learned that their previous workplace had been toxic and that my approach to suggesting ideas, unintentionally, mirrored the dynamics my peer had worked so hard to escape. I also realized I wasn't involving them enough in decisions that impacted their territory. Once I understood this, I explained my intentions, making it clear that we were working toward the same goals and that I didn't realize how awful I was coming across. I guess one could say that we had a heart-to-heart of sorts – and I like to think we saw each other more as humans after that. That one conversation completely changed the way we worked together, and from that point on, collaboration became much smoother.

During our long walk winding through the streets of a quiet American city, I also gained valuable insight into our regions' cultural differences and recognized that my approach needed some adjustment to be effective there. I also started to make more of an effort to be more inclusive in my planning. In return, they made an effort to give me the benefit of the doubt when I came off as aggressive and inconsiderate.

We achieved great things during our time at the company. Yes, we still fought – but we had more respect for each other. I ended up liking them as a person, and I like to think they liked me, too.

Some ways to be more likeable

While not an exhaustive list, here are some ways to be likable - or at least to take the edge off some of your more prickly spots. Note that I make no guarantees that these will work for everyone, nor do I guarantee these will work in contexts outside of the workplace (for example, I'm not sure your pet cat will take to these techniques, but you are welcome to try).

- **Don't talk down** - Make the program easy to understand by breaking down technical jargon into relatable, non-technical language. Use visuals, analogies, and storytelling to ensure everyone, regardless of their expertise, feels confident in understanding the process and outcomes of your tests. However, respect their intelligence and experience.

- **Actively listen** - Show genuine interest in their perspectives and, as previously mentioned, align your program's objectives to address their needs, making them feel heard and valued. Ask open-ended questions to encourage deeper discussion and clarity. Remember to reflect and paraphrase what you hear to confirm your understanding. Resist the urge to jump to solutions or dismiss their concerns too quickly - doing so can limit creative thinking and narrow the conversation.

- **Communicate proactively** - Keep stakeholders informed with regular updates that are clear, concise, and relevant. When you share information with folks, it makes them feel appreciated and helps prevent unwanted surprises. Experimentation, by its very nature, challenges beliefs and, potentially, authority. Sharing results with sensitive parties before broadly communicating them is in your best interests - no one likes being blindsided. The same goes for celebrating successes. Pre-sharing them with sensitive parties reinforces that you feel their input is important and gives you an opportunity to acknowledge their contributions. Finally, remember to recognize challenges and provide a transparent roadmap of the next steps, as they often spark commentary and feedback.

- **Celebrate collaboration** - Highlight and credit the contributions of team members and stakeholders involved in the program. By recognizing their efforts, you create a sense of shared ownership and foster goodwill, encouraging them to support and advocate for the program.

- **Deliver on promises** - Your word must be your bond. Be dependable even on the smallest of promises. If they cannot trust that you will do what you say you will do, they will trust nothing else.

Be the agent of positive change

Beyond being likeable (which honestly should be table stakes for life in general), it's in your best interests to build your brand around a **commitment to innovation and delivering results that matter**. Each test you run is an opportunity to prove that you make decisions grounded in data, not guesswork, and focused on driving real impact. Sharing wins—or even lessons from setbacks—positions you and your program as the go-to resource for smart, evidence-based strategies. All this boosts your credibility as someone who **brings value and clarity** to the table. Here are some approaches to consider:

- **Keep an upbeat attitude** - Not only will this
  improve your productivity, but it will also attract
  others to work with you and inspire confidence in
  others. Positivity is contagious, and in a field where
  win rates are like batting averages - you will swing
  and miss more than you hit home runs - every bit of
  positivity helps. Just remember not to go
  overboard. There's being upbeat, and then there's
  toxic positivity. Toxic positivity is when someone
  insists on staying overly optimistic and dismisses
  anything negative, even when those concerns are
  valid.

- **Be collaborative and avoid being a lone wolf**
  - Model what it looks like to combine clear
  communication, thoughtful planning, and
  flexibility. Stay curious, ask meaningful questions,
  and bring others into the process. When you're
  transparent—celebrating wins, owning mistakes,
  and giving credit where it's due—you set a bar for
  teamwork and **integrity**.

- **Just do it** - Pick a small handful of things to
  improve within your control, then just do it. For
  example, starting a group chat to discuss a topic or

speaking up when you feel the conversation is meandering. Often these little things are already on others' minds but they refrain from taken action out of fear of either looking silly or poking a bear. But if you can demonstrate that you are focused on moving things forward, you will be more appreciated than you know. Little moves add up.

Over time, as your program delivers more results, people will see you as a leader who **drives change** and pushes the company toward smarter, more efficient decisions - and start to **emulate you**.

Be the expert leader

When I was a child, I was the only one who could set the VCR (some of you may need to Google what those are) in my family. That made me the electronics expert in the house and the go-to resource for all electronics purchasing decisions. While electronics were seen as an important thing to have in our homes, no one else cared to understand how to operate them.

In the workplace, most people don't get statistics, so helping others navigate that world will not only further build your credibility but also position you as an expert — and people tend to trust experts. Not to toot my own horn, but I still help my mother pick appliances.

However, while you'll want to be seen as the expert, you also don't want to be a bottleneck where everyone comes to you for *every little thing related to experimentation*. Did I mention that I still help my mother pick appliances? Unless you start levelling up others, you will find yourself spread too thin - unable to advance experimentation at your organization beyond the basics.

This is why you need to be seen not just as an expert but as an **expert leader**. Whenever possible, make an effort to **level up others** so that they can self-serve their own experimentation needs. Explain your experiment designs, walk through your results evaluation methodology, and share your decision-making approach. Slowly introduce them to themes like Frequentist, Bayesian, CUPED, and the difference between statistical and practical significance. The more fluent everyone is in experimentation, the easier your life will be and the more performant your company will be - and with a little luck, everyone will remember who made that a reality.

Tactfully showcase your experience

Most people are reassured by a leader who has been there and done that. It gives them confidence in the leader's decisions and perspectives. So, while it is good to always have a plan B, it is better to present it in a way that shows you aren't shaken by an unexpected experiment result. Whenever you have the opportunity, share how a situation reminds you of something you've seen in the past and how you dealt with it. However, what if you don't have that kind of experience? How do you build or maintain trust, then? Here are a few ways:

- **Be an authority by association** - Reference books, podcasts, and/or industry leaders in your conversations - and do it confidently. You might not be seasoned, but that doesn't mean you can't be knowledgeable.

- **Ask smart, probing questions** - Ask questions that help you to understand the problem space better. Understand the opportunities and challenges. Asking *why* will be your best friend. Hopefully, as you probe, this will remind you of an experience or reference you can mention that will help a conversation.

- **Noodle on it -** However, if after all this, you aren't still unable to draw upon anything, simply say that you will review your notes, give the situation some thought, and get back to them shortly - which sounds infinitely better than saying, "Wow, I've never seen *that* before. Huh!? Geez. I dunno what to say."

Be a winner ASAP

As we all know, first impressions count. You'll want others to perceive your program as a net positive to the company - so finding a win, *any win*, is important within the first 90 days of your program. Don't underestimate how early wins of any scale frame you and your program in stakeholders' minds.

Early wins prove to others that you can take action, get results, and create momentum. They associate you with progress and smart decision-making. They get leadership and other teams excited, making it easier to push for bigger experiments later. In short, they prove you're not just testing for the sake of testing—you're driving real impact.

However, perhaps you are in a situation where you don't have all the resources you need to execute a test. In this case, highlight material opportunities backed by data and information that illustrate potential gains or averted losses. Be vocal. If you can't score the goal, be the coach that highlights the winning play.

Control the message

Controlling how your program is communicated helps ensure it's valued. **As early as you can**, establish a regular cadence of updates that shares progress, showcases your points of view, celebrates wins and learnings, and demonstrates that your program is working on things your stakeholders value. Be transparent and *tactful* about any challenges, highlighting how the program partnered with others to navigate them without blaming individuals. Shout out teams and co-workers whenever positive things happen to increase excitement around your program and engagement with your communications. But how do you get these messages out? Here are a few ways to consider:

1. **Internal newsletters -** Send regular updates with insights, success stories, upcoming experiments and any trends you are seeing. Consistency is key— make your updates as dependable as the program itself.

2. **All-hands or team presentations -** Use meetings to share big wins, explain your process, and build excitement. Revisit key concepts periodically to keep everyone, including new hires,

in the loop.

3. **Collaboration tools or dashboards** - Platforms like Slack, Teams, or dedicated dashboards are great for real-time updates and discussions. They keep your program visible and make it easy for others to engage.

4. **Surveys** - Use surveys to gauge how people feel about the program. Share the results, create action plans to address feedback, and keep everyone updated on your progress. Accountability builds trust.

5. **Champions** - Internal ambassadors or champions can contribute to and amplify your communications. You don't have to put everything on your shoulders.

6. **Onboarding** - While more challenging at larger companies, try to be involved in the new employee onboarding process. Show the new folks the ropes.

Don't let others control the narrative.

Start doing this *immediately* because, like it or not, others may try to shape the narrative to benefit themselves - sometimes intentionally, sometimes not. CRO is all about optimization, which often means exposing areas that aren't working as they should. And guess what? Those areas are usually owned by people who don't want to be in the spotlight for the wrong reasons. Some may try to get ahead of the story, spin it in their favour, or even shift the blame when things don't go well. Controlling the narrative early ensures you stay in charge of the story—not them.

Advice from CRO experts

Personal branding, feedback and change management

Ellie Hughes

Head of Consulting at Eclipse

in /in/ellieexperiment/

As an experimenter working in a large product organization, your feedback process and your internal personal branding within the company are intrinsically linked to each other. If you're not iterating how you work and what you do, then nobody's really going to trust you to take an iterative approach with them.

You need a really robust framework in place to tell people about how you run your experimentation program, but here's the thing: When you're hired into a business, you often come in with this huge expectation that you'll build this amazing program from scratch. What actually happens is your ivory tower theory hits the reality of the product organization, and they're not ready for it.

One of the key steps is building your personal brand for experimentation and rolling that out as part of a wider change management program to drive the experimentation business. The second any new product manager comes into the business, you need to sit down with them, engage them, and let them know who you are and what you represent. You're there to support them, but don't push your perfect idea of experimentation straight away.

Instead, wait until they come to you, but be proactive about building your personal brand through founding chapters, creating centres of excellence, and demonstrating how experimentation can validate ideas and improve customer loyalty.

Whether your business is B2C or B2B, you need to be out there presenting on showcases, running lunch-and-learns, and creating this real cultural movement around what you're doing. Find every single format where you can demonstrate the practical nature of experimentation and how it relates to what they do. It's about finding ways to insert experimentation into things people are already doing rather than trying to force a perfect theoretical model on them.

Don't forget tech

Lucas Vos

Senior Conversion Specialist at RTL

in /in/lucasfjvos/

While the commercial and marketing stakeholders are, most of the time, a lot more demanding than your stakeholders from Tech, don't forget them. At RTL Netherlands, we learned that quite the hard way.

While being too busy with accelerating experimentation and launching more and more experiments after the other, we blew our reputation with the developers by breaking a very important customer flow on one of the busiest days of the year. Outside of the very angry phone call and other responses we got, it resulted in a completely removed A/B testing platform, so we could not experiment for months. It took almost half a year with a lot of lobbying to get it reimplemented because the tooling wasn't trusted anymore. Even after that, experimentation for a few years afterward was the first to be (falsely) blamed for incidents.

So, don't forget your developers and other tech colleagues as important stakeholders and let them influence the quality of experiments.

Building your reputation

Ton Wesseling

Experimentation Coach, Founder & Host of The Conferences known as Conversion Hotel and Experimentation Island, as well as The Experimentation Culture Awards
🌐 *tonw.com*

Apply for awards, get interviewed for blogs and podcasts, and present at conferences. Once your co-workers see you mentioned externally, it greatly boosts your internal reputation - especially award nominations. And, of course, save some budget to buy ads for these interviews targeted at people who work at your company! Be a guerilla marketer!

Chapter 2 summary

- Building a strong reputation for your experimentation program early on is crucial—it shapes how stakeholders perceive it and helps navigate company dynamics.

- But success isn't just about data and strategy; likeability matters. People support those they enjoy working with, so focus on clear communication, active listening, and celebrating collaboration.

- Trust and credibility come from showcasing experience and delivering results.

- Control the narrative by regularly sharing updates, highlighting wins, and ensuring technical teams are on board.

- A respected, well-communicated program becomes indispensable, making it easier to influence change, secure resources, and drive impactful decisions across the organization. Strong relationships foster long-term buy-in.

Chapter 3
Optimize for progress

When the honeymoon is over

So, you've gotten people on board with your experimentation program, the updates are flowing, people love working with you, and you've got all your roadmaps and goals set. Bravo! Time to sit back and just run the program, right? Not so fast.

In your first year, you can expect the following:

- Issues with your testing platform. Inevitably, something will stop working, and things will grind to a halt.

- To go through a rough patch of few to no wins. All the early hype will start to fizzle out, and continued program costs will raise eyebrows with leadership.

- The shiny newness of your program will wear off, and leadership will start making everyone chase the next big thing, like AI.

- Test results contradict what a HiPPO (Highest Paid Person's Opinion) predicts. It will take some serious finesse to handle the moments when your program ruffles a few feathers at the top.

The CRO Excitement Cycle

There have been times throughout my career when I felt that I was flying high with an experimentation program - only to come crashing down shortly after. For instance, at one company I joined, my arrival was announced with great fanfare as if I were the game-changer they had been waiting for. Excitement surrounded every test, and our work was held up as the gold standard.

But the company had been around for a while, and just like at every other long-established organization, all the obvious optimizations had already been explored. Experimentation had to shift from going after big wins to squeezing out incremental improvements, and the process became a grind. Excitement quickly turned into pressure when quarterly targets were missed. That pressure only grew when leadership realized the experimentation program wasn't going to generate billions overnight, and preventing losses wasn't something the board cared to hear about.

Once the initial hype faded, the company's focus shifted to the next trendy buzzword, and experimentation would only be valued again if it uncovered immediate revenue opportunities or silver-bullet solutions. Learning stopped being a priority - only big wins mattered.

At another company, my experimentation program thrived under a president who was a strong advocate for data-driven decision-making. But when she left, priorities changed overnight. Data and measurement took a backseat to flashy new initiatives, and experimentation was no longer the company's focus.

Under the new regime, there was always the threat of constant budget cuts hanging over us. I kept thinking to myself, "*How do you put an ROI on learning?*" Every day, I felt uncertain about the importance of my role despite scrambling to prove my value daily through the sheer volume of work and increased visibility. I managed to keep the program alive for a few more years. However, leadership eventually shifted most of its resources toward personalization, and anything not directly tied to that was cut—including experimentation (don't try to make sense of this; I know I couldn't).

So what should you do when your program loses its new-program smell? How do you keep the momentum — and more importantly — how do you maintain the support of senior leadership?

Let's explore a few ways to survive the storm.

Highlight your program's constant progress

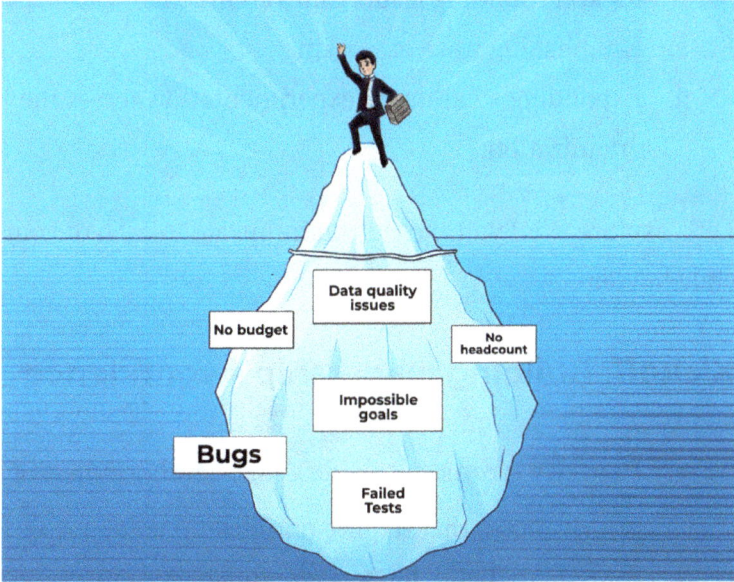

There is more to your experimentation program than just winning.

Consistently demonstrating **progress** is essential if you have any chance of keeping your program afloat - not just at the start but for the long haul. Stakeholders want to know that their continued investment is still making a difference, even if the wins aren't constant. The kinds of progress you should showcase depend on what phase your experimentation program is in. As a reminder, experimentation programs evolve through the following phases (if you need a refresher, review Chapter 1):

1. Kickoff: Building leadership's confidence
2. Establishing ways of working
3. Expanding a culture of experimentation across the organization.

Let's explore what you should communicate to each of your stakeholders.

Kickoff: Building leadership's confidence

- **Priority Areas** — Provide a high-level overview of priority areas that require optimization along with the data to justify it (Bonus points if you can estimate lost revenue.) Everyone loves someone with a firm direction. Don't be wishy-washy. You may get pushback, but be reasonably firm unless someone raises something truly compelling.

- **Defined roadmaps** — Share a clear roadmap for the program, including milestones for software implementation, initial tests, and long-term outcomes. Is your roadmap in flux because of other teams? (Fun fact: It will.) Consider sharing updates to your roadmap regularly.

- **Vendor selection updates** — Share the progress in selecting an A/B testing platform. Showcase how it aligns with your company's goals and teams' needs. Highlight agreements. Highlight discoveries. Highlight how vendors differ. Share which you've selected — and why — repeatedly. You'll be surprised how often you'll be asked why you selected the vendor that you did. Also, don't be too surprised if stakeholders you invited to help choose the vendor *but never attended a single meeting* complain about your decision. Remember to document the process. You'll thank me later.

- **Stakeholder engagements** — Communicate how you've secured buy-in from key teams (e.g., product, marketing, engineering) to hold other teams accountable and demonstrate you are having all the conversations you should to ensure that experimentation operations run smoothly. If needed, highlight areas where you need support (in a respectful way, ideally).

- **Training plans** — Share plans for onboarding teams on how to use any A/B testing software effectively, formulate hypotheses, etc. Share news about workshops and/or training sessions. Consider reporting on what percentage of the company has been trained to demonstrate experimentation adoption.

- **Technical set-up milestones** — Celebrate achievements like integrating your testing platform with your tech stack, setting up tracking, or completing API configurations. If applicable, call out areas your product or analytics teams need to validate.

- **Test environment readiness** — Report on preparing environments for experimentation, such as aligning with QA or deploying staging environments.

- **Pilot experiments** — Share updates about any simple tests during implementation that verify the software setup and demonstrate early functionality. Celebrate if data flows through properly.

- **Quick wins** — Deliver low-lift, impactful results that address visible problems, like minor UX improvements or quick conversion rate boosts.

Establishing ways of working

- **The experimentation intake form** - This is especially true if you operate in a model with centralized experimentation operations. Creating an intake form for experiment-related work will help you keep track of activities and help potential experimenters think through their experiments thoughtfully. Try not to make the form so long that potential experimenters shy away from submitting ideas or so short that you have to follow up every submission with dozens of clarifying questions and hours of meetings.

- **Documentation and templates** — Develop and share experiment templates, playbooks, or best practices that teams can use once the platform is fully operational. Pro tip: Ask your A/B vendor for some pre-existing materials.

- **Test insights** — Share lessons learned from early tests, even if they're not wins, to show how the program is shaping smarter decisions and highlight areas for process improvement. Consider challenging the status quo or generally accepted opinions. While it is tempting to mention every detail, try to stick to the most critical pieces of information - including screenshots if you have any.

- **Insights Repository** - Create a repository of test results, insights, and methodologies that empower other teams to make data-driven decisions. Consider including regular learning lookbacks — for which you look back at a period of time and try to identify patterns that others can learn from. Consider a robust tagging and naming system that considers themes, areas, and owners because you will definitely forget the names of experiments.

Expanding the experimentation culture

- **Scaling efforts** — Highlight how the program is expanding by running more tests, involving additional teams, or tackling larger projects. Consider mentioning your program's coverage/support of functions, channels, and KPIs.

- **Long-term impact** — Report on cumulative metrics, such as total revenue uplift, reduced churn, or customer satisfaction improvements over time. Consider using a global holdout here to get a good read, as A/B test results are rarely additive.

- **Cultural shift** — Highlight how experimentation has become a key part of organizational decision-making and influencing broader strategies. The more others see that important decisions require an experimentation component, the more likely others will seek to run experiments to further their projects.

- **Portfolio wins** – Show the program's ability to consistently deliver a mix of high-impact wins and valuable insights across various initiatives, including moonshots.

- **Tool ROI** – Demonstrate how the investments in tools have paid off (or are paying off) through generated wins, averted losses, hours saved because of better analytics, faster test launches, or increased testing volume. It is in your best interest to proactively surface this information before you renew your tools (or before the annual budget process starts) and to ensure it reaches those holding the purse strings.

- **Cost avoidance** – Share examples of how invalidating ideas early prevented wasted resources or failed initiatives (in a tactful way, of course).

- **Program adaptability** – Highlight the ability of your program to pivot based on company goals,

market trends, or other new challenges. Showcase
how you are keeping the program relevant and
impactful. Highlight these pivots as they happen.

- **Efficiency gains** — Demonstrate time or cost
  savings through streamlined processes, reduced
  approval cycles, or reusable experiment templates.
  These may be hard to measure precisely, but focus
  on a consistent measurement method rather than
  precision. The trend is more important than
  exactness.

Highlight blockers and your efforts to overcome them

When things don't go as planned, it's easy for the
experimentation program to take a lot of blame. While I
am not suggesting that you finger-point or deflect blame if
blame is justified, I do strongly suggest that you highlight
whether your program is set up for success or if there are
areas that need addressing.

Be sure to highlight *bottlenecks* like limited engineering support, insufficient analytics capacity, political red tape, or less-than-ideal goal setting. Clearly identifying these pain points helps stakeholders understand what's holding the program back or how it could achieve even greater impact with the right support.

Raise this awareness early; if your program fails to deliver ROI, you will have already started conversations to remove some of these blockers, demonstrating to your leadership that you are working on making progress - buying you some time.

It goes without saying that if you can secure more resources and unblock a bottleneck, report on the progress gained from the investment regularly to encourage even more investment.

Here are a few tips on identifying and framing your asks.

- **Map out your workflows** — Map out all of your program's key workflows with a particular focus on those that depend on other teams to get things done. List out all the times when you need to get buy-in or have to convince others to get on their roadmap, etc. and take note of which ones are consistent bottlenecks.

- **Fix problems under your control** - Optically, it's in your interest to ensure that you're not throwing rocks while living in a glass house. So, as you map out your workflows, you will identify times when your program or team is the source of issues for others. Maybe your less rigorous QA process causes problems for engineering. Perhaps your end-to-end optimization conflicts with ongoing marketing work. Proactively addressing these issues on your own will go a long way toward building good faith when you start asking for help later.

- **Ask for help** - This is probably the most obvious tip. The squeaky wheel gets the oil. Never assume your leadership or stakeholders are monitoring your program very closely. Unless you say something, everyone will assume everything is fine — or worse, won't care if it fails. The following are ways to frame requests that increase your chances of getting support:

- **Align with a strategic initiative** - Most of the time, a company is focused on a few strategic initiatives for the year. If you can frame your request in a way that supports at least one of those, it makes it easier for a senior leader to add a bullet point to a slide about their department's progress towards those goals and, in turn, support you. In short, never underestimate the power of making a senior leader look good.

- **Quantify unrealized potential** - Estimate the value of a roadmap of opportunities the company is missing out on. For instance, you could say something like this: "This backlog of high-potential experiments could drive an estimated $500k in incremental revenue, but we don't have the engineering support to realize them." However you phrase your ask, it should be:

- **As specific as possible** - Instead of vaguely saying that you'll do 'things,' highlight specific initiatives or projects that will be unlocked. Senior leadership generally wants to see a clear return on investment as early as possible, and being detailed with your proposal builds trust that their investment won't go to waste.

- **Ground the incremental revenue within a timeframe** to make it feel real. I.e., instead of saying that a test could generate $1M, say that it could generate $1M in three quarters. Again, addressing leadership's need for a clear path to positive ROI.

- **Compare against benchmarks** - Use industry or company benchmarks to show how additional resources would help you achieve goals. For example, "Teams in similar organizations run twice as many experiments because they have dedicated analysts and developers, leading to faster decision-making and higher ROI." You'll get brownie points if you can name your competitor.

- ○ **Highlight efficiency gains** - Propose how more resources would drive efficiency. For example, "Investing in a dedicated experimentation analyst would free up engineering time, allowing us to test more ideas without hindering other initiatives."

- ○ **Pilot resource use** - Sometimes, a trial can help warm up stakeholders to further investment. Suggest running a pilot program with the desired resources to prove the value. For instance, "By borrowing a developer for one quarter, we could launch a high-priority experiment to demonstrate immediate ROI."

- ○ **Team up with a stakeholder** - Highlight a stakeholder's opportunity that would benefit directly from more support. For example, you could say, "The product team has identified this experiment as a potential key revenue driver, but their current bandwidth limits their ability to execute." Bonus points if the stakeholder owns a very important OKR. Double bonus points if they have political power.

Promote the mindset of progress over perfection

Evangelizing the power of a progress-oriented mindset is essential to maintaining buy-in for and ensuring the long-term success of your experimentation program. A company whose culture focuses on progress embraces change, treats challenges as opportunities, and prioritizes learning over perfection. This mindset encourages teams to take calculated risks, act boldly, and continuously refine their approaches. It replaces fear of failure with curiosity and adaptability - **recognizing that mistakes are part of the process.** Long story short: They test more with less drama.

Here are a few ways to encourage that mindset in your organization.

Framing matters.

Glamorize grit

Statistically, most tests don't result in a positive result. So, it is not unusual for conversion rate optimizers to iterate on a test several times to produce a win. This process could take weeks, months or over a year. While this can be frustrating, every unexpected test outcome presents an opportunity for you to lead.

As the experimentation program leader, demonstrate how people should handle an inconclusive or negative result and set the tone for the program. Consider sharing how you diagnosed the problem and identified potential iterations until you secure a win or strategically pivot toward something better. Showcasing these moments of grit, even if modest or imperfect, is invaluable in demonstrating how experimentation is the right way to drive results because it replaces guesswork with data-driven insights, continuous improvement, and risk mitigation based on real user behaviour. As you uncover win after hard-fought win, others emulate you.

Also, don't limit yourself to grinding on big tests. Take the same approach to ones that need less development, too.

Promote purposeful next steps

Having a pre-existing plan for what happens after you receive the results of an experiment—whether it's a win, loss, or inconclusive result—not only keeps things moving and prevents stagnation but also emphasizes the importance of **testing with purpose**. Without clear next steps, momentum can stall; work can get bogged down by endless cycles of analysis, and the project risks introducing

HiPPO-biases. Predetermining actions ensures that every test drives progress, shifting the focus from just gathering data to creating meaningful change. It makes the process feel intentional, impactful, and efficient.

Don't underestimate the mighty button design test.

Let me illustrate this with a simple example. Before running a test, you can decide that if the test satisfies its predetermined success criteria to roll out the winning variation immediately. Similarly, if it fails, you will refine the hypothesis and launch a follow-up test. Even an inconclusive result can prompt valuable actions, like revisiting user insights or testing alternative variations. By outlining these steps *ahead of time*, you avoid analysis paralysis and impulsive decisions while at the same time showing stakeholders that each experiment serves a purpose and fits into a larger strategy.

Documenting an experiment's next steps is crucial for keeping everyone **aligned and accountable**. Remember, people tend to hold onto their ideas—even the bad ones. Often, once the test results are in, stakeholders may unconsciously suggest next steps that align with their personal agendas (aka unofficial KPIs) rather than with the company's best interests - this is natural. Having a clear and documented plan helps keep things objective and ensures the program maintains its integrity. After all, what's the point of experimenting if you ignore the evidence and do what you want anyway? That said, be tactful and know when to back down - especially with senior leadership. Sometimes, you have to choose your battles wisely.

Only act on things that matter

Sometimes, keeping focus can be challenging.

As most of you know, when it comes to experimentation, it's not enough to rely solely on statistical significance to guide your decisions—you also need to determine a level of **practical significance** or a "**threshold of caring**" to ensure you act only on results that matter. We do this because while statistical significance tells you whether an observed effect is unlikely due to chance, it doesn't address whether the effect is meaningful in a real-world context. In other words, **not all positive results are worth the time,** and you need to **know when to move on**.

While it is natural to want to implement every seemingly positive result, one should always seek to do the following:

- **Avoid wasting resources** - Implementing changes that lack practical significance consumes time, money, and energy without delivering meaningful benefits. By ignoring less meaningful results, you can focus resources on initiatives that have a real impact. Wasting even a day of engineering effort that will result in changes that won't be noticed is not a good look - especially if there is a lot of high-priority work going on.

- **Prioritize high-value changes** - Acting only on results that surpass your threshold of caring reinforces to your organization that they ought to be biased towards bigger swings if they want to see bigger results.

- **Avoids over-optimization** - Chasing tiny, insignificant improvements can lead to over-complication or frequent changes that confuse users or disrupt workflows without any tangible benefit. There is a point when you've sharpened a knife beyond what is considered practical. If you've put in a boatload of effort and your results continue to be unremarkable, move on - unless it's a critical strategic priority, move on.

- **Reduce noise in decision-making** - Ignoring low-impact results helps maintain clarity and focus. Decisions based on minor, **insignificant changes can lead to inconsistency and decision fatigue** over time. Don't underestimate the chaos you introduce when you start paying attention to every little blip of data. You'll find yourself debating and defending actions constantly. Save yourself the stress.

- **Foster strategic thinking** - Evaluating test results through the lens of practical significance and against a threshold of caring encourages a broader, long-term perspective rather than reactive decision-making.

Some of you may ask, *"What's the harm?"* I'll take any improvement I can! While I get it, let's consider this example.

Imagine you somehow ran a statistically significant experiment with an expected relative lift in revenue per visitor (RPV) of just 0.1% (just go with it). Let's also say your current RPV is $5. That means the expected lift would be $0.005 per visitor (we're ignoring the confidence interval stuff here for simplicity). To generate just one extra dollar, you'd need 200 visitors.

Now, let's assume you're getting 1 million visitors per week (just go with it). Implementing this change would bring in $60K per year. If you're working with that level of traffic, $60K annually isn't likely worth celebrating. In fact, *it may cost* $60K to implement this change in production.

Furthermore, don't underestimate the ability of senior leaders to lose track of all the nuances of test results. Because they'll only remember whether there was a win and not necessarily the *size* of the impact, **they'll expect**

to see improvements to the business sooner rather than later. If you keep implementing tiny wins that don't impact the company, leadership will question your capabilities.

But how do you decide on a threshold of caring? There's no clear-cut answer, but here are things to keep in mind:

- **Understand the optics** - Choose a threshold that looks "good" against those goals compared to other initiatives when annualized. For instance, an extra $52K per year looks nice when your company only generates $1M annually but not when it makes $1B monthly.

- **Consider opportunity costs** - Every decision has a trade-off. The resources spent implementing a minor improvement **could be used for more impactful projects**. Your threshold of caring should reflect the opportunity cost of pursuing low-value changes.

- **Review historical data** - Review past A/B tests to see what levels of KPI improvement have historically led to meaningful results. Use these insights to set a realistic and impactful threshold.

- **Involve your stakeholders** - Collaborate with team members and decision-makers to agree on a meaningful threshold. This prevents disagreements later and ensures alignment across the organization. With that said, you ought to go into those conversations with an opinion based on the above points in case they have no strong opinions.

In summary, without this additional filter, you risk acting on changes that don't make a tangible difference to your business, which wastes time and resources on trivial outcomes - establishing a practical significance threshold forces you to define what success truly means for your goals and reinforces the idea of pragmatism, and strengthens the credibility of your experimentation program.

Figure out what's not worth your time quickly

When dealing with complex conversion funnels - those with multiple stages, branches, or feedback loops - it's not always clear where to focus. Add aggressive goals or timelines to the mix, and things get even trickier. In these situations, I rely on quick, targeted tests to eliminate low-value ideas quickly so I can focus on what matters.

In situations where I have sufficient traffic, instead of sinking weeks into a single idea, I simultaneously test multiple distinct but lower-effort changes using a multi-armed bandit (MAB) approach that automatically shifts more traffic to better-performing variations. This allows me to rule out the weakest options early and hone in on areas with real potential. I'll then run bigger A/B tests based on the winner of the MAB.

Sometimes, I like to run quick tests on low-effort but noticeable changes. They're not always the final version of what I have in mind, but they help me challenge fundamental or risky assumptions. These tests could be fake door tests—like showing users a button for a feature that doesn't exist yet—or a Wizard of Oz test, where we would manually simulate a feature to make it seem automated, etc. I'm not aiming for practical significance here; I'm just looking for signs of interest—some heat. If something gets a reaction, I'll dig deeper with proper A/B tests on the variants that moved the needle.

By filtering out low-impact changes upfront, I save time, budget, and effort by avoiding rabbit holes and only doubling down on high-value optimizations that actually move the needle.

Dealing with HiPPOs and HiPPOcrites

Dealing with HiPPOs (Highest Paid Person's Opinions) can be tricky because they hold a lot of power and influence. While they are often vilified, **you need them**. They control the money, authority, and influence to make things happen. The challenge? HiPPOs are used to having their ideas implemented without question, while experimentation focuses on data-driven decisions that can disrupt traditional hierarchies. In other words, **experimentation challenges authority**. As the owner of an experimentation program, your goal is to build a learning roadmap based on data, evidence, and research—not just the whims of someone used to getting their way. However, an experimentation program can threaten a HiPPO's position if not carefully managed.

To complicate matters, there's an especially annoying type of HiPPO to watch out for in experimentation: **the HiPPOcrite**. This is probably the most dangerous kind of

HiPPO - the one with *some* past A/B testing experience
who thinks their ideas are obvious wins (usually shared in
a demeaning tone) and should take priority. Yet, at the
same time, they'll tell you to "follow the data," "challenge
everything," and "do what's right for the business,"
creating a mix of contradictions and headaches. They will
think poorly of you if you don't test their ideas. If you test
them and they lose, you tested them improperly and
should try again. What a mess.

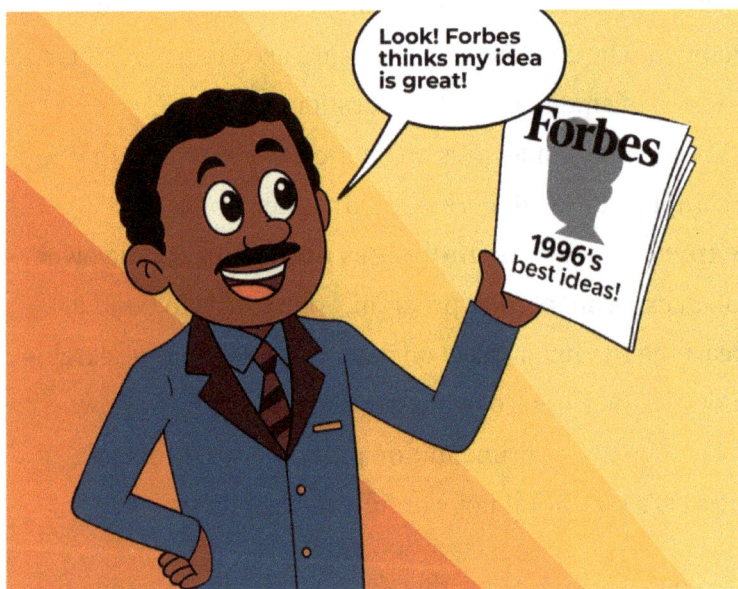

Not all ideas stand the test of time.

Many years ago, I joined a new division tasked with improving conversion rates across multiple channels. I was brought in to "turn every stone," "work across functions," and "make things happen."

So, I proposed countless ideas backed by research and secured buy-in from all the major teams. Still, senior leadership began dismissing all my suggestions - often favouring old, dusty tactics that worked for them at a previous company. They would justify their approach by referencing outdated Forbes articles from well over a decade ago. It soon became apparent that they weren't looking for fresh, data-driven insights; **they wanted someone to validate their ideas**.

Whenever I landed on an idea senior leadership had once considered themselves, I suddenly needed less supporting evidence, and the idea was declared brilliant. (Fun fact: They weren't. They often flopped pretty hard.)

It goes without saying: working with senior leadership requires *a careful balance*. While you want to run your program with integrity, many senior leaders only want you to prove them right. Not to mention that you probably want to keep your job too - tricky stuff.

Regardless of the kind of HiPPO you work with, here are a few tips on keeping them happy and involved while ensuring their influence doesn't derail your program or your employment. (Good luck!)

- **Acknowledge their input respectfully -** Validate their contributions to maintain goodwill, and steer the conversation toward data and evidence to prove them out. For example: "That's an interesting idea—let's see if the data supports it."

- **Anchor discussions in data-driven processes** - Use clear, visual data and reference the established experimentation process to depersonalize decisions. *Your process* may recommend that you avoid running a test or call a test variant a loser, *not you*. It's important to focus on the data and evidence and not on whose idea it was.

- **Educate without being condescending -** Explain concepts in approachable terms and afford HiPPOs the grace of already knowing them. For example, I like to say, "As you probably are aware, that's a common pitfall we've seen before, but here's how we can avoid it through testing."

- **Involve them selectively** - While I encourage you to involve HiPPOs in experimentation (e.g. during brainstorming or reviewing results), beware of wild flailing, especially from HiPPOcrites if these sessions involve many people. Discussions often go sideways when HiPPOcrites ask participants to chase down random information to appear in control, validate their half-baked ideas, or ensure that someone else's idea is wrong. Similarly, beware of getting too deep into the weeds on low-priority or meaningless things (i.e. bikeshedding).

Fun Fact: The term **bikeshedding,** also called **Parkinson's Law of Triviality**, derives from a story in which a committee once spent far too much time debating the design of a bikeshed instead of focusing on a vastly more complex nuclear power plant project because the bikeshed was easier to understand. You'll often see this type of thing when people argue about logo sizes or button colours instead of the information architecture of a page.

You can avoid bikeshedding by doing your best to keep everyone's focus on the needed high-impact decisions, setting clear agendas ahead of meetings, and tactfully shutting down unnecessary chatter over minor details.

- **Leverage a prioritization framework to show how accommodating you are** - A prioritization system (e.g., ICE: Impact, Confidence, and Effort - see Chapter 5 for more frameworks) can help you illustrate to a HiPPO how other ideas have more opportunity than theirs. However, before you do that, consider demonstrating that you trust their experience and let one of their ideas jump the queue. If that idea wins, the HiPPOcrite will be an ally forever. If their idea loses, it inserts doubt into their mind the next time they try push their idea ahead of others. Another approach to consider is to show your roadmap and ask the HiPPOcrite which deliverable should be deprioritized. Many HiPPOcrites balk at the idea of being wrong in a public way.

- **Handle HiPPOcrite's failures tactfully -** In the case that a HiPPOcrite's idea doesn't perform well, showcase the learnings in a positive light. It's in your interest to have HiPPOs doubt their opinions - not to make them look bad. You still need their support.

- **Have HiPPOs sign off on next steps before an experiment launches -** I mentioned this before, but clearly define and document success metrics upfront so everyone understands *and agrees on* how test results will be evaluated and acted upon. This reduces the chance that a HiPPOcrite introduces subjective interpretations of test results. I like to say, "Let's define what good and bad looks like and capture how we will follow up in either situation." I get as specific as possible and hold people to these decisions - including the HiPPO.

- **Routinely tie the work back to the problems you are trying to solve -** As you dive into problems and run countless tests, leaders can easily lose track of what you are doing. Connecting your work, learnings, and eventual wins back to the company's problems in all your communications reinforces that you're a strategic partner in driving the organization forward. It also encourages feedback, allowing you to course-correct if needed.

- **But choose battles wisely** - Not every idea from a HiPPO is bad or needs a direct challenge. If their suggestion won't cause harm, consider testing it to build a collaborative brand and earn their trust for the future.

Cross their T's and dot their I's

When starting an experimentation program, it's natural to want everything to be perfect right away—but that's not where your focus should be. Instead, prioritize making experimentation as simple and useful as possible for your early adopters at the beginning so they can understand the value of the process and of prioritizing progress over perfection.

For example, at the beginning of your program, instead of forcing potential experimenters to fill out elaborate forms, handle that yourself to make things easier for them. You may take on other tasks like scheduling meetings or sharing results with stakeholders on their behalf. That said, what you should never skip is walking your stakeholders through the experimentation process. They should live the experience of hypothesis creation, learning from experiment results (no matter what they are) and iterating on them.

As people get comfortable with the process, gradually shift responsibilities to them. By then, they'll appreciate the value of the program and be more willing to take on those tasks. Avoid waiting too long, though, or they will get used to having you do everything for them, and you will become a bottleneck as your program expands. This gradual handoff not only smoothes the transition but also shows you're invested in their success. Eventually, early adopters will share their positive experiences with others, naturally encouraging them to also run experiments - helping the program to grow.

Advice from CRO experts

Consistent communication is critical

Nathan Pedrozo

Senior CRO at Better Collective

in *in/nathanpedrozo/*

Consistent communication plays a critical role in driving momentum, particularly when rolling out change, like training employees to experiment. Keeping stakeholders informed on a regular basis helps create a sense of ownership and involvement. It's a key part of building organizational support for experimentation; when people feel connected to the process, they're more likely to buy in.

The focus on tangible outcomes — such as process improvements and measurable impacts – creates a direct link between training efforts and business value. It's about demonstrating how these efforts translate into real, meaningful results. By showcasing these successes, you're not only celebrating wins but reinforcing behaviours and mindsets you want to see across the organization.

Last but not least, the concept of accountability is crucial.

When employees see their progress tied to larger goals and understand how their contributions drive the broader mission, it fosters a sense of ownership and urgency. This transparency accelerates adoption and helps embed experimentation as a core organizational behaviour.

Juicy discoveries take time

Claire More

CRO Manager at Enavi
 /in/claire-more-599713214/

If there's one thing I've learned in my career as a CRO Specialist, it's that successful CRO programs take time. It takes time to get solid "wins" and learnings from tests before winning streaks happen. Testing low-hanging fruit in the beginning while you ramp up targeted research efforts can be great, but there is a necessity to understand that programs typically need 3+ months before you get to the juicy discoveries.

Things to consider when asking for engineering resources

Rommil Santiago

Founder of Experiment Nation

in */in/rommil/*

I appreciate the irony of putting myself in one of these CRO Expert boxes. However, this is important.

*Every experimentation program wants more engineering support. But before you ask, consider whether you need to test on **multiple tech stacks** and whether there is enough **continuous** work for them.*

Suppose you need to work on wildly different tech stacks (e.g. different platforms, frameworks, languages, etc.). In that case, finding an engineering resource with enough knowledge to work in all your environments will be challenging. Anyone you find that is able to do so is more useful elsewhere. Remember: every company wants its best engineers to work on the most important things - and that's unlikely to be on experiments.

Furthermore, few experimentation programs produce enough work to keep an engineering team occupied all day, every day unless the program is scaled up and mature (if that's your case, then why are you reading this book?)

Ultimately, if you can get full-time engineering resources, that's great! But be prepared to maximize them as soon as you get them because they will be drafted when other parts of the business face a crunch.

Reframing "losing"

Tracy Laranjo

On-Demand CRO Strategist & Coach

in */in/tracylaranjo/*

Stakeholders tell me they appreciate how I reframe "losing" tests by estimating the monetary losses we avoided by not implementing the change. This approach resonates for a few reasons:

1. *It makes the value of testing easier for stakeholders to understand by communicating the avoided impact with tangible business metrics (like revenue).*

2. *It makes the value of testing easier for stakeholders to understand by communicating the avoided impact with tangible business metrics (like revenue).*

3. *It shifts the narrative from fear of failure to celebrating informed decision-making, reframing failure as a necessary part of progress that we can*

learn from to move forward.

4. *It demonstrates transparency and trustworthiness by openly sharing all results, even the less favourable ones.*

Chapter 3 summary

- Sustaining an experimentation program requires ongoing momentum and stakeholder support.

- As excitement fades, highlight progress over perfection - show efficiency gains, cost avoidance, and long-term impact.

- Communicate roadblocks and consider framing resource needs in terms of revenue potential.

- Handle HiPPOs (Highest Paid Person's Opinions) by balancing the validation of their ideas with data-driven decisions.

- Position experimentation as a strategic tool for smarter decision-making.

Chapter 4
Welcome feedback

Feedback is the lifeblood of improvement

Getting feedback from stakeholders is key to fine-tuning and improving your experimentation program. Sure, criticism can sting a bit, but seeking it out helps you spot bottlenecks, uncover opportunities, and make sure everyone's on the same page with your goals. Being open to feedback shows you're listening, builds trust, and proves you're serious about the program's success. It also strengthens your processes and lets stakeholders know their input matters, laying the groundwork for long-term collaboration.

Here are some ways to collect and use first-hand feedback effectively:

- **Conduct retrospectives -** Regularly schedule feedback sessions or retrospectives with stakeholders, including key decision-makers. Use these discussions to explore what you should continue doing, what you should start, and what you should stop. Even if senior stakeholders don't attend, inviting them signals your proactive approach. Document the findings, prioritize critical concerns, and assign action items to demonstrate that their input drives meaningful action.

- **Send surveys** - Distribute surveys to gather feedback on communication clarity, process efficiency, and potential obstacles. Include open-ended questions to get more detailed replies, then summarize and share the key takeaways along with your action plan to address recurring themes. For bonus points, incorporate questions from an experimentation maturity assessment (many can be found online) to track the evolution of your program over time.

- **Create feedback loops within updates** - Add a section in your regular progress updates explicitly asking for feedback. This helps collect more real-time feedback. If you wait too long to collect feedback, stakeholders often forget about opportunities and pain points they've encountered.

Acting on feedback through Champions

Your job isn't to come up with all the best ideas - it's to act on the best ideas.

Program Champions are engaged advocates who play a pivotal role in the success of your experimentation program. They deeply understand A/B testing, support its adoption, and know how to overcome challenges. Acting as connectors between the experimentation team and the organization, Champions also help you succeed by:

- **Providing honest feedback** - Their close involvement allows them to offer candid, actionable insights about strengths, weaknesses, and opportunities for improvement.

- **Driving adoption** - Program champions are instrumental in implementing changes effectively. Their familiarity with the day-to-day makes them well-positioned to suggest realistic solutions and pilot adjustments within their teams. This ensures that changes are practical and pressure-tested before wider rollout.

- **Building momentum** - Sharing their positive experiences inspires others to get involved. Furthermore, because they aren't part of the experimentation team, they give your program more credibility.

- **Advocating for resources** - Champions can influence decision-makers to secure additional funding, tools, or personnel to support the program's growth.

At one company, I made it a point to book meetings with every product manager to explore data, understand their challenges, and find ways to answer key questions through experimentation. But more often than not, meetings were rescheduled, ignored, or attended without any real follow-through. It was a frustrating time.

Then, a product manager joined the company at a reasonably senior level—and everything changed. She came from an organization that truly valued experimentation, and she was a game-changer. At every opportunity, she encouraged teams to test their ideas, challenging plans by asking, "Where's the supporting experimental evidence?"

With her as a Program Champion, the company ran more tests, iterated faster, and built a culture of experimentation. She spread this mindset across her team, and as team structures evolved, those she trained passed on the same practices to others.

She and I had weekly one-on-one meetings to review goals, track progress, and tackle roadblocks. She actively shared experimentation updates through Slack, team meetings, and leadership discussions, ensuring the process stayed top of mind.

Her impact was undeniable. With her support, we tested extensively, saved significant costs, and brought in a substantial number of new customers.

To get the most out of Champions like these, keep them engaged with retrospectives, progress updates, and regular feedback sessions. Publicly recognize their contributions to keep them motivated and strengthen their connection to the program.

Dashboards

As many of you know, an experimentation program dashboard is a powerful feedback tool for program owners and sponsors to monitor the program's performance and drive continuous improvements. By consolidating key metrics, insights, and operational information in one place, the dashboard provides a clear picture of the program's health and impact. Regularly reviewing this data ensures that the program evolves to meet its objectives while maintaining a strong foundation for growth. However, deciding what goes into a dashboard isn't always straightforward. Let's explore this further.

The dashboard challenge

Dashboards: So simple, yet so hard.

Unfortunately, as much as you are the expert in this field, your stakeholders will have their own opinions on what should be on the dashboard. Here are some of the hurdles you may face:

- **Diverse stakeholder expectations** - Different stakeholders have varying priorities, making it difficult to create a dashboard that satisfies everyone. For instance, marketing might prioritize campaign performance, while product teams focus on feature adoption.

- **Data overload** —Stakeholders often request numerous metrics, which can result in a cluttered dashboard that dilutes actionable insights. Striking the right balance between comprehensiveness and simplicity is a common hurdle.

- **A lack of shared vocabulary** - It's not uncommon for different groups to call stages of a funnel different things or call different stages the same thing. Taking the time to create a dictionary or glossary with exact definitions will save you a lot of headaches later. There's no place for fuzziness here.

- **Nothing ties back to business goals** - If the dashboard metrics don't clearly tie back to any business objectives or the goals of the experimentation program, stakeholders may question its value or misinterpret its insights. Dashboards must drive action towards something of business importance.

- **Varied levels of data literacy** - Not all stakeholders have the same understanding of data. Designing a dashboard that's accessible to non-technical users while still providing depth for data-savvy stakeholders is a significant challenge. Consider legends and leveraging visualization beyond simple tables. And if you have the time, present and walk stakeholders through the dashboard.

- **Timeliness and accuracy** - Stakeholders often demand immediate insights, but experimentation results require time to achieve statistical validity. Managing expectations around real-time reporting versus accurate, actionable results is crucial. Adding visible notes and the time and date of the last refresh helps - especially if the dashboard will be distributed broadly.

Ways to get everyone on board with your dashboard

Getting leadership and other important stakeholders to agree on what's included in a dashboard (let alone for an experimentation program) often requires a bit of strategic maneuvering. One smart move is finding **influential allies within, or close with, the leadership team—** those who already see the value of experimentation or are big on data-driven decisions. Share your vision (and concerns) with them early, get their feedback, and turn them into advocates. When already respected voices back your proposals, it's much easier to win over the rest of the team.

Another common yet effective tactic is **building consensus through compromise**. Identify the non-negotiables for each leader and look for overlaps or shared priorities. Design the dashboard to emphasize these commonalities while leaving space for secondary metrics that address individual concerns. Presenting it as a flexible tool that evolves based on input can help diffuse conflicts and encourage buy-in from all sides. I often like to say, "This will be the first revision. We'll revisit next month to improve on it."

Another effective political tactic to align stubborn leaders is to **highlight the opportunity cost of inaction or misalignment**. Frame the conversation around what's at stake if a dashboard isn't agreed upon - such as missed insights or slower decision-making. Emphasize how delays could hinder the organization's ability to compete, innovate, or respond to market changes. Position the dashboard as a tool that mitigates these risks and ensures everyone is working from a consistent, reliable source of truth. This can help reluctant leaders see alignment as not just beneficial but necessary for success.

Metrics to avoid

Beyond the messy politics, when designing an experimentation dashboard, knowing what metrics to exclude is just as important as knowing what to include. Some metrics may seem relevant at first glance but can muddy the waters when it comes to decision-making. These often fall into three categories: **vanity metrics**, **incomplete data**, or **overly granular detail**. However, while they might not belong on the main dashboard, some of these metrics could still have a place in deeper analysis or specific team reports. Let's explore the categories you should **not** include on an experimentation program dashboard and why:

- **Vanity metrics** - This should not come as a surprise. But I include this for completeness. Things like total website visits or raw app downloads might look impressive, but they don't tell you much about the success of your experiments. These metrics lack context and don't provide actionable insights, so they're just noise on a dashboard meant to focus on driving decisions. OK, now we have the obvious behind us. Let's move on to some meatier metrics to exclude.

- **Incomplete data** - Avoid showing early results or metrics based on incomplete data. Including numbers that aren't statistically valid can lead to premature decisions or confusion. The dashboard should only display metrics that give a clear and reliable picture of experiment outcomes. **Do not underestimate** people's tendency to remember incomplete information and run with it - especially if it's in their favour. I once shared data from an experiment that showed a lift early on - like 3 days in. Despite the results flattening out afterward, word of the early lift spread so fast up the chain that I couldn't catch up with it and decisions were made. Even after trying to correct leaders' understanding of the final outcome, I was dismissed because the decision had already been made. Did I mention never to underestimate people's tendency to run with incomplete data that is in their favour? It's a thing. Trust me.

- **Overly granular metrics -** Tracking click-through rates for every single button variation in an A/B test isn't dashboard-worthy. **Leaders and stakeholders need a big-picture view**, not a deep dive into every detail. Save the nitty-gritty for deeper reports or team-level analysis. Make sure you are not missing the forest for the trees.

Cover your ass metrics

Let's touch on some KPIs you *should* add to your program dashboard. Your future self will thank me later.

- **Test velocity (number of tests run per period)** - Some of you may be saying to yourselves, "Rommil! That's a vanity metric!" Hear me out. Test velocity shows how frequently experiments are being launched — something stakeholders are keen to know in a program's early days, especially as they'll likely brag about this to senior leadership. Later on, a drop in velocity could indicate resource bottlenecks, inefficiencies in workflows, shifts in strategy, or a lack of stakeholder engagement, signalling the need for intervention.

- **Win rate (Percentage of tests producing positive results)** - Some of you may be saying to yourselves, "Rommil! Experimentation isn't only about winning!" Hear me out. A consistently low success rate (i.e., in the low single digits) may indicate poorly defined hypotheses, inadequate research, or flawed test design. Identifying patterns here can guide adjustments to your pre-test processes or training. Use this metric to justify coaching and workshops aimed at helping others design better experiments.

- **Test coverage** - Some of you... (I'm just kidding, but hear me out all the same). Track whether experiments are evenly distributed across critical areas such as product, marketing, and customer experience. You typically should see more tests around the most strategic areas and a fairly even distribution otherwise. Having several areas without active testing isn't unusual, as some areas are very challenging to test from a technical or legal perspective. However, beyond that, spotty coverage might indicate missed opportunities, underdeveloped relationships with that area of the business, or an overemphasis on low-impact areas - all of which suggest a reallocation of effort. Consider taking a portfolio approach where test coverage addresses all the major functional areas, OKRs, and/or levels of risk (e.g. moonshot, discovery, iteration, etc.) A well-considered portfolio is a good way to show how strategic your program is.

- **Revenue generated / losses averted** - This one, admittedly, is a little tricky at the start of a program. However, it is a great way to show the program's impact on the bottom line and a subtle reminder to keep seeking impactful tests. Be sure to adjust your numbers so they account for a full year of traffic.

For your backpocket

Not everything belongs on a dashboard. However, some helpful information to track *somewhere* for a rainy day are:

- **A list of metrics you can impact and meaningfully influence** - This can be a game-changer for running an effective experimentation program. Not all metrics are created equal—some are more actionable and directly tied to decisions you can make, while others might be harder to move or less relevant to your goals. By tracking historical performance and analyzing past experiments, you can establish benchmarks for realistic "success" for each metric. Additionally, this approach enables better decision-making when designing experiments. If you know a metric, such as average order value, is highly sensitive to changes in pricing or promotions, you can focus efforts there rather than wasting time on metrics that historically show low responsiveness. Over time, this kind of tracking creates a feedback loop where you continuously refine your understanding of what drives impact, leading to more effective experimentation and better alignment with business goals.

- **Segment performance** - While your dashboard might focus on overall results, deeper insights into how specific user groups respond to experiment variations can be invaluable for long-term learnings. For example, an experiment might have neutral overall results but reveal a strong positive impact on a particular customer segment(s). **Simpson's Paradox** is a phenomenon that happens when a trend appears in separate groups but reverses when the groups are combined. Monitoring these metrics separately ensures you don't miss opportunities to personalize or optimize for key audiences.

- **Time-to-launch (Average duration to start a test)** - If launching tests takes too long, it may highlight bottlenecks in approval processes, tool limitations, team capacity issues, or declining experimentation priority. Reducing this time accelerates learning cycles and boosts program efficiency.

- **Experiment completion rate (Percentage of tests that run to completion) -** A high number of incomplete or abandoned tests suggests issues like inadequate traffic allocation, shifting priorities, insufficient QA or unclear objectives. Incomplete experiments ought to be the exception, not the norm. If you're not completing many experiments, hold a retrospective and root-cause analysis to identify patterns. More often than not, you'll find the cause in short order. If needed, don't hesitate to request additional resources (See Chapter 3 on ways to ask).

- **Decisions influenced -** Ultimately, experimentation is a tool to inform business decisions. An ideal program influences every major decision the company makes. As part of your intake, consider capturing all the business decisions a given experiment should influence and start keeping a tally of them. Being able to share that your program generated millions of dollars and influenced dozens of business decisions is an enviable position.

Feedback you should ignore

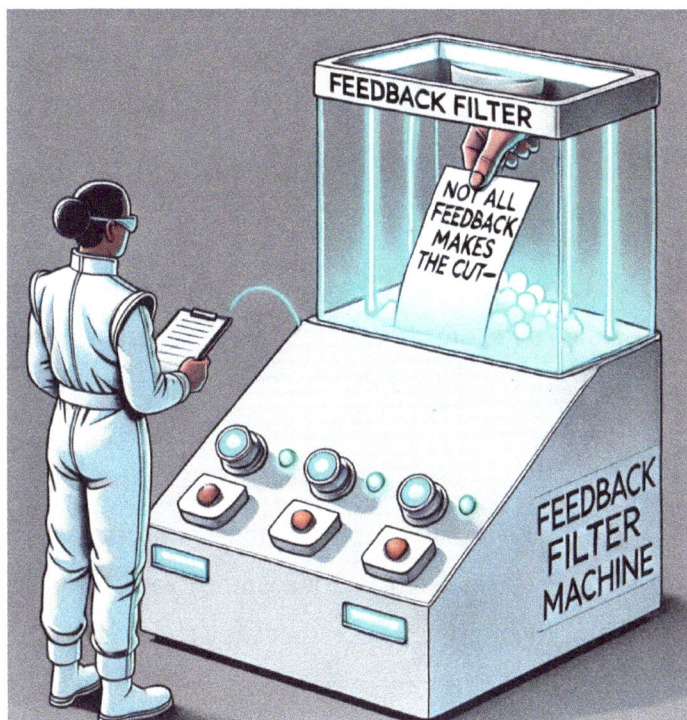

Not all feedback is meaningful. Learn to know the difference.

Not all feedback about your experimentation program is worth acting on, and that's OK. Sometimes, people offer opinions that aren't backed by data, or they might suggest changes based on something they saw on LinkedIn. Their feedback might focus on vanity metrics or unrealistic expectations, like wanting overnight results. It's important to filter out the noise and prioritize feedback that aligns with your program's goals and is grounded in actionable insights. Remember, saying "no" to the wrong feedback helps keep your program focused and effective. Here are some of the kinds of feedback you (probably) should ignore:

- **Misaligned objectives** - If the feedback comes from stakeholders who don't fully understand the goals or purpose of the program, it may push you in a direction that conflicts with your objectives.

- **Resistance to change** - Some feedback may stem from a fear of change or discomfort with experimentation itself rather than legitimate concerns. This kind of resistance shouldn't derail a well-thought-out strategy. Take the time to understand their perspectives and try to ease their concerns as best as you can. Examples of this kind of feedback are, "How can we avoid creating unnecessary work?" or "How can we only run experiments we know will win?"

- **Conflicts with best practices or expertise -** When feedback contradicts established best practices, proven methodologies, or your team's expertise, it's worth considering why the input doesn't align and whether it adds value before acting on it. More often than not, you'll need to educate while being mindful of not condescending to them. However, if you find that they strongly don't agree, consider revisiting the topic later when things have cooled down.

Watch out for red flags

Sometimes, feedback comes in subtle hints that suggest your program is not valuable anymore. Changes in organizational priorities or leadership communication can often signal potential risks to an experimentation program's funding. Recognizing these red flags early can

You will need to pivot quickly when you smell changes coming.

help you take proactive measures to address concerns and protect the program's future.

Here are some key warning signs to watch out for:

- **Shifting priorities** - If after your experimentation program struggles to find a meaningful win for a prolonged period, and you notice leadership scrambling to find ways to cut costs or boost revenue immediately, your experimentation program may be in trouble. Your program may have been seen as a path toward aggressive revenue growth, but leadership has given up on it.

- **Radio silence from leadership** - If leaders stop showing up to meetings, don't ask questions, or give vague feedback, it's a sign your program is not a priority. When they're not engaged, the program risks being forgotten or deprioritized.

- **Budget cuts in related areas** - When teams or tools tied to experimentation—like analytics or marketing—start seeing budget freezes, it's a red flag. Leaders might be quietly shifting resources elsewhere, which could mean your program is next on the chopping block.

- **Skepticism about results** - If leadership starts questioning the program's impact or doesn't seem convinced by the results you're sharing, it's time to reframe how you communicate value. A lack of confidence in the program is a red flag.

- **Disappearing advocacy -** If the leaders or champions who used to rave about the program suddenly go quiet or leave for whatever reason, that's a bad sign. Without vocal support, it's harder to justify its value to others.

- **Leadership turnover -** With new leaders come new priorities. If someone new steps into a decision-making role, they might not see the program's value.

- **Gut-driven decision-making -** If leadership starts making (more) decisions based on instincts instead of data, the program could lose its relevance. It's tough to push experimentation when the culture shifts to guesswork.

- **Cutbacks to innovation -** If the company pulls back on big ideas, R&D, or other forward-thinking projects, experimentation could get lumped into the "non-essential" category. Linking your program to operational efficiency and quick wins might save it.

- **Heavy investment into innovation -** On the other hand, if your company starts investing very heavily in innovation areas like personalization or AI, it often comes at the expense of other programs, such as experimentation.

If you find that your experimentation program is at risk, **act fast**. With a little luck, you can turn things around by (re)proving the program's value and (re)aligning it with what the company and stakeholders care about. Here are some actions you can take to protect your program and get everyone back on board:

- **Show them the money -** Pull together the previously mentioned data on how the program has driven revenue, saved costs, loss averted or improved key metrics. Share specific wins that tie directly to the company's goals and make the program's value impossible to ignore. Do this repeatedly. If possible, set up a global holdout to help demonstrate your program's impact.

- **Reconnect with leadership** - Schedule quick updates with key decision-makers. Keep it short and focus on uncovering more ways how the program can better support their priorities.

- **Tie testing to new goals** - If the company's priorities have shifted, adjust your focus to match. Whether it's cutting costs, increasing efficiency, or boosting revenue, get ahead of it and make it clear how experimentation can help achieve those goals.

- **Get some quick wins (again)** - Plan and launch a few high-impact, fast-turnaround tests that deliver noticeable results. Nothing silences doubt like an obvious win.

- **Reengage champions** - Get your program advocates back in the game. Share data, successes, or updates with them, and ask for their support in spreading the word about the program's impact. In return, share the spotlight with them.

Advice from CRO experts

Earning recognition with dashboards

Ton Wesseling

Experimentation Coach, Founder & Host of The Conferences known as Conversion Hotel and Experimentation Island, as well as The Experimentation Culture Awards
🌐*tonw.com*

My best trick has always been to email/post weekly updates of a screen recording of myself walking through the dashboard and explaining learnings. Creating a 2 to 3-minute video with my face in there. It is easy to process and great for generating recognition in larger organizations.

Suddenly, everyone knows you are someone who is helping to grow the business (so focus on positive news also).

Feedback isn't criticism

Tim Thijsse

Sr. Lead Customer Experience Optimisation at OrangeValley

in /in/timthijsse/

Feedback isn't criticism; it's an opportunity to continuously improve systems and experiences. The key is transforming insights into concrete actions that enrich your strategy.

Chapter 4 summary

- Feedback is crucial for refining and strengthening your experimentation program. It helps identify bottlenecks, improve processes, and build stakeholder trust.

- Actively seeking feedback—through retrospectives, surveys, and ongoing updates—ensures your program remains relevant and aligned with company goals.

- Champions within your organization can be key allies, driving adoption, piloting changes, and advocating for resources.

- Dashboards are powerful tools for communicating program impact but must balance simplicity with depth to satisfy different stakeholders.

- Be mindful of red flags signalling leadership's waning interest and proactively showcase experimentation's value through clear wins and business impact.

- Not all feedback is useful—filter out noise, focus on constructive insights, and align suggestions with best practices.

- Ultimately, experimentation thrives in a culture that values progress, iteration, and continuous learning.

- Keep communication open, highlight successes, and ensure your program remains a strategic asset, not just a nice-to-have.

Chapter 5

Other snags, gotchas, and tips (Oh my)

Navigating other political snags and gotchas

Just another day of managing stakeholder expectations.

If you've made it this far, you (hopefully) know that experimentation isn't just about running tests and analyzing data—it's also about navigating the complex web of organizational politics. In this section, we'll dive into some of the trickier political snags and gotchas you might encounter that didn't fit elsewhere in this book, along with strategies to manage them without losing momentum—or your sanity.

But first, I wanted to share a real-life example of how company politics can get messy and why the strategies I'm about to share are crucial to implementing an experimentation program as smoothly as possible.

I once took on a position at an international software company, and my role was to drive growth and be the glue bridging several siloed teams: marketing, product, and analytics - but things didn't work out as planned. Each team's leader would whisper into my ear about how they wanted me to spy on and influence the other leaders. Meanwhile, our general manager would pit his staff against each other through conflicting goals. Unsurprisingly, our goals were misaligned and unrealistic. It was the epitome of a toxic workplace.

I quickly learned that keeping everyone happy without seeming biased was a challenge. We had big goals but were falling short, and trust between teams was nonexistent—no one wanted to collaborate. Being spread across different time zones and countries only made things more complicated. Ultimately, real progress was only made when lower-level team members found ways to succeed despite the conflict between their superiors - but it was slow and hard-won.

In the end, they shut down the entire division. Despite having a few wins along the way, it was too little, too late. On a positive note, while it was a painful time in my career, I did learn many valuable lessons.

Avoiding inter-stakeholder conflict

We touched on this earlier. Experimentation prioritization frameworks help you decide which ideas to test first, ensuring your efforts are focused on experiments with the most potential impact. Since not all ideas are created equal, prioritization frameworks provide a structured way - based on data and evidence - to objectively evaluate test opportunities based on factors like expected value, feasibility, and alignment with business goals. While no prioritization framework is completely free from manipulation, a well-chosen one keeps your experimentation program efficient, focused, and, most importantly, effective.

Some popular frameworks include:

- **ICE (Impact, Confidence, Effort)** - This straightforward framework scores each idea based on its potential impact (i.e. the impact on each user), your confidence in its success, and the effort required to implement it. ICE is simple and works well in fast-moving environments where speed matters more than deep analysis.

- **RICE (Reach, Impact, Confidence, Effort)** - Similar to ICE, RICE scores ideas based on their potential impact, your confidence in their success, and the effort required to implement them. However, RICE introduces an additional factor — "Reach," which measures *how many people* an idea will affect within a given period. This makes RICE more suited for scenarios where the breadth of impact is a key consideration, offering a more granular prioritization method compared to ICE.

- **PIE (Potential, Importance, Ease)** - Also similar to ICE, this framework focuses on the potential improvement an idea offers, its importance to the business or customer experience, and how easy it is to implement. PIE often works well in product-focused teams that aim to balance big wins with quick wins.

- **EVA (Expected Value Added)** - This framework calculates the potential return on investment for each experiment. It's ideal for teams that have enough historical data to estimate outcomes accurately. To be honest, I've never used this framework, nor have I ever heard of someone using it, but it didn't rhyme with ICE, so it felt deserving to be included here.

- **MoSCoW** - This framework helps you decide what matters most in a project. It sorts tasks into four categories: **Must-haves** (essential), **Should-haves** (important but not critical), **Could-haves** (nice to have), and **Won't-haves** (not needed now).

More complex prioritization frameworks also exist, like CXL's PXL, which emphasizes factors such as the visibility and traffic a treatment will receive. However, the right framework for your program depends on your company's political landscape and decision-making style. In low-complexity environments where stakeholders are aligned, simpler models like ICE or PIE often work well.

However, in organizations with competing priorities, strong personalities, or rigid approval processes, a detailed and more data-driven framework may be necessary to build consensus and justify decisions. In politically complex environments like these, my rule of thumb is to have at least **one criterion per troublesome stakeholder**. This way, they can each feel heard.

Whichever framework you choose, agreeing on one upfront sets clear expectations, turning prioritization into a collaborative process that focuses on objective criteria and avoids unnecessary conflict.

Tests can have unexpected blast radiuses

A big mistake many make with experimentation is focusing too narrowly on a single outcome or small part of the business. The reality is that every experiment you run can have ripple effects across multiple functions—sales, marketing, customer support, engineering, other business units, you name it. By limiting your focus, you're missing a golden opportunity to showcase the broader value of your program.

This is why you should evaluate your experiments using something called an **Overall Evaluation Criterion** (OEC). Sounds fancy, but it's just a consistent set of metrics you use to measure the impact of each test from all angles. Instead of only looking at, say, a lift in sales, your OEC might also consider other aspects important to your business, such as how the test affects customer support call volume, marketing efficiency, or fraud volume.

When you take this holistic approach, your experiments matter to a lot more people. Instead of being just a side project for one team, experiments become a source of strategic insight across departments. Experiment results stop being "just data" and start becoming fuel for big-picture debates - debates that help shape the direction of the company. And the more people there are who care about your experiments, the harder it is for your experimentation program to be ignored or deprioritized.

Talk to leaders across your organization to select the best metrics to include in your OEC, biasing towards those that — based on historical data — you feel the company can impact the most. Revisit this on an annual basis to coincide with when your company sets its annual goals to keep your OEC relevant. Finally, don't be afraid to update it if you feel they aren't driving the right conversations or decisions.

So think big, show off the ripple effects, and turn those test results into something everyone wants to talk about.

Pushing back on Legal

Eventually, you will end up testing something that could be touchy from a legal point of view. Typically, this is around pricing, promotions, or sensitive information. A lesson I learned many years ago is if Legal is giving you a hard time, remember three things:

1. **Legal doesn't own business decisions** - Ultimately, someone will own the business decision of a test by weighing its potential benefits against its costs and risks. Find that person and explain the situation. The business owner will often push legal to find a path forward by sharing more context.

2. **Quantify the risk to determine if it is acceptable** - Always proactively quantify potential risks. Legal is not able to quantify the risk of an experiment. Sometimes, what seems like a big deal to them at the beginning turns out to be only a few thousand dollars' worth of risk. Quantifying this risk helps business decision owners make the right call.

3. **Explain that things are temporary and reversible** - Sometimes, legal doesn't understand that A/B tests can be turned off and be temporary. Sharing this detail often eases a lot of concerns.

Training

One of the most beautiful—and challenging—aspects of experimentation is that it sits at the crossroads of multiple disciplines. It touches on UX, analytics, statistics, project management, communication, and (as I hope this book emphasizes) workplace politics. Unfortunately, expecting others to pick up all these skills overnight is unrealistic. As you introduce newcomers to the practice, patience will be your greatest asset. That said, there are some areas where it's best not to go too deep.

Statistics

Statistics is one of those tricky subjects—people either get it or pretend to. Kidding aside, for those without prior exposure, statistics can feel overwhelming. Instead of diving into the weeds, stick to high-level concepts and let tools or statisticians handle the details. This ensures consistent interpretation of results while lowering the barrier for others to embrace experimentation. Most people won't (usually) refuse a helping hand, so stepping in to handle the tricky calculations can go a long way toward fostering adoption.

But watch out for dangerous misinterpretation where decisions are being made off of misunderstanding of results. In these cases, don't hesitate to correct folks (politely) if they are using terms incorrectly. The usual suspects include: statistical significance, confidence, confidence interval, and MDE. (I.e., brush up on these.)

Some people just can't grasp statistics - and that's OK.

Rethink workshops

Workshops are an obvious way to train people, offering visibility and a collaborative environment. But they come with challenges:

- **Scheduling headaches** - As interest in experimentation grows, repeating the same training for larger groups becomes time-consuming.

- **Mixed skill levels** - Balancing content for beginners and advanced participants often results in wasted time or confusion.

- **Dominant participants** - The most outspoken attendees tend to monopolize attention, leaving quieter participants behind.

To address these issues, I would recommend holding at least one workshop at the beginning to get to know people, have live discussions, and gain visibility. Afterwards, consider blending in the following approaches:

- **High-level documents** - Create simple guides that explain the basics without overwhelming detail. Most learners just want to understand the process and identify knowledge gaps.

- **Training videos -** Video tutorials give students something to revisit and eliminate the need for exhaustive note-taking.

- **1:1 sessions -** After learners review the basics, schedule individual meetings to address specific questions. This maximizes impact and helps refine your materials.

- **Live demos and examples -** Providing hands-on examples or demo sites makes concepts more tangible and easier to grasp.

- **Supplemental articles -** Share relevant articles to reinforce key ideas.

- **Surveys for feedback -** Send post-training surveys to identify gaps and improve future materials. Use scoring systems to highlight areas needing attention.

- **Smaller groups** - Sometimes, you don't need everyone in the room. You can often get what you need done with a smaller team and share the notes afterward. I like to invite non-critical people as optional so no one feels left out, but it gives folks an out if they have more pressing matters to attend to.

Show training progress

Sharing the progress of employee training is a powerful way to build momentum for your program and demonstrate its growing value. Regular updates can highlight key achievements, such as the number of employees trained, departments engaged, or improvements in the quality and frequency of experiments being run. Showcasing these milestones signals that the program is gaining traction and helps reinforce the importance of experimentation to leadership and stakeholders. Focusing on tangible outcomes, like how training has led to more impactful experiments or streamlined processes, also connects training directly to business value.

Building a testing platform – rarely worth It

Building an in-house experimentation testing platform may sound enticing. After all, it promises total control, customized features, and independence from vendor fees. However, unless your company has *unique experimentation needs* (hint: you probably don't) that enable a strategic advantage (hint: it's unlikely) that cannot be met by existing solutions (hint: slim chance), building a platform is rarely worth the effort. Even in such cases, the challenges and **costs of maintaining an in-house solution almost always outweigh the benefits**, making this a path only beneficial for the rarest of scenarios.

As someone who has overseen the building of a very modest server-side testing platform, the biggest challenge of building an in-house platform isn't the initial build itself (though that in of itself is a lot harder than many think) but rather keeping the platform running efficiently over time. Privacy regulations like GDPR, CCPA, and cookie deprecation require constant updates to ensure compliance. Falling behind on changes like these can lead to invalid results and legal risks. Similarly, staying relevant in the fast-evolving A/B testing space demands regular innovation in personalization, AI-powered analysis, and data warehouse native analytics, just to name a few. Without a dedicated team of *top-tier* engineers and product managers, your platform will struggle to keep up with these trends. TL;DR: You'll end up paying many times more for a solution that is many times worse than what vendors offer.

But, let's say you had world-class talent; **the opportunity cost alone** of dedicating them to maintaining a custom platform is high. Their skills are often better applied to driving your core business objectives rather than reinventing infrastructure that third-party vendors have already perfected. Established tools offer robust, scalable, and constantly improving solutions tailored to market demands—without the burden of development and upkeep.

The way I like to frame this for those who are hellbent on building a platform is that it's like wanting to add a few numbers together but insisting on reinventing Excel.

If your company struggles with building complex products, buy.

Picking an A/B testing platform

Assuming you've wisely avoided the rabbit hole of building your own A/B testing platform, picking the right one might seem simple—just go for the tool with the best features, right? Not so fast. In reality, this decision can be surprisingly political. It impacts multiple teams - engineering, marketing, and analytics - and everyone will have opinions about what works best for them. Your job isn't just to choose the right tool; it's also to make sure everyone feels their concerns are heard and that they feel the choice benefits the company as a whole.

Here's the tricky part — as the expert, you likely have a clear idea of what's best for your experimentation program. Unfortunately, other stakeholders may not share your priorities and could push for a less-than-ideal solution. While it's crucial to respect their needs, you also need to be ready to stand your ground—after all, the success of the program ultimately rests on *your shoulders*.

The stakes are high (as high as corporate life can get for a business experimenter, at least). If the company chooses poorly, you could end up with a tool no one wants to use, a frustrated engineering team, or, worst of all, a stalled program that never gets off the ground. The following sections cover ways to get the people who matter on your side.

Get the budget owner's buy-in

Start by identifying who controls the *budget* for your experimentation platform - is it the product leader, marketing director, or head of engineering? Once you know, the key is to frame the value of the tool in a way that speaks directly to them. Let's be honest—they're not losing any sleep over the experimentation program itself. Their priority is finding something that makes their job easier or helps them hit their goals - within budget.

Did you find the perfect experimentation tool with advanced stats like CUPED or Sequential? Great! But if engineering owns the budget, you'll need to emphasize things like SDKs, strong security, and seamless implementation. Engineering teams love clean code, efficient processes, and systems that won't slow them down, so show how your tool fits right in with their priorities. If marketing is footing the bill, shift your pitch. Highlight how the tool can generate more MQLs, shorten the time to production, and deliver solid ROI - all the things that help them hit their targets. Remember, be ready to demonstrate how the tool won't disrupt anyone's workflow.

Here are some ways to help you frame your interactions with them to increase the odds of getting their buy-in:

- **Start with discovery, not decisions** - Before you even look at platforms, talk to your stakeholders. What are their pain points? What features do they absolutely need? Does engineering prefer certain integrations, or does marketing have a wishlist of analytics capabilities? These conversations aren't just about gathering requirements—they're about building relationships and showing that you value their input. Bonus: You'll avoid nasty surprises later when someone says, "Why didn't you ask us about this?"

- **Frame the platform as a shared solution** - Nobody wants to feel like a decision was forced on them. Frame the platform as a solution that supports *everyone's* goals. For example, emphasize how it will help marketing optimize campaigns, make engineering's life easier with a streamlined setup, or empower analysts with better reporting tools. The more each team sees the platform as solving their specific problems, the easier it'll be to get their buy-in.

- **Don't skip the trade-offs talk** - No platform is perfect, and someone will have to compromise. Be upfront about trade-offs, but focus on the benefits for the company as a whole. For instance, "This platform might not have the deepest analytics tools, but it integrates seamlessly with our existing tech stack, which saves engineering weeks of setup time." Position the decision as the best overall fit (biased towards the needs of your budget-owner, of course), even if it's not a perfect fit for every team.

- **Pilot before committing** - Whenever possible, pilot the platform with a small group of stakeholders (including the budget owner) before rolling it out company-wide. This not only gives you a chance to see how it works in practice but also gives those involved a sense of ownership in the decision. If the pilot goes well, you'll have early champions who can vouch for the platform's value and help bring others on board.

- **Think about the (somewhat near) future:**
  While you are trying to solve the problems at hand,
  you need to also consider where your company is
  headed. Is it overhauling its tech stack? Is it shifting
  away from client-side testing? Is it looking to
  double test velocity? While no one can predict the
  future, understanding potential future needs can
  save you a lot of headaches down the road.

Rubrics help people feel heard

Like prioritization frameworks, using a rubric to pick an
A/B testing platform brings structure and objectivity to a
decision that can easily become subjective and political.
Whether your company is marketing-led, engineering-led,
or product-led, your rubric should reflect these dynamics
while ensuring that the requirements of all stakeholders
are considered.

As you should expect by now, **start by identifying the
priorities of each team involved**—such as security and
scalability for engineering, speed and ease of use for
marketing, or flexibility for product teams—and build your
rubric to evaluate vendors across these dimensions. Of
course, lean slightly toward the priorities of the team that

owns the budget, as their buy-in will be critical to moving forward. However, if you predict that the budget-owner's needs will be counter to what your program needs, you may want to consider making the majority of the rubric cover the dimensions of other stakeholders *in an attempt to "outvote" the budget owner.* (While not my preferred approach, sometimes you have to play hardball.)

Then, **create a scoring scale** for each criterion that reflects how well a vendor meets your expectations. A simple scale works well, such as 0, meaning the vendor doesn't meet the requirement, and 5, meaning they exceed your expectations. Criteria might include aspects like ease of integration, reporting capabilities, customization options, support quality, and cost. **Be clear and specific** about what each score represents so your evaluations are consistent and objective across vendors.

It's also essential to **define your nonnegotiables -** mandatory criteria for your program's success. For example, in an engineering-led company, data security or API flexibility might be nonnegotiable, while in a marketing-led company, it might require intuitive, self-service test creation. Any vendor scoring below a certain threshold on these must-haves (e.g., a 3 or below) should be eliminated from consideration immediately, regardless of their performance in other areas. By clearly identifying these deal-breakers, you streamline the evaluation process and avoid wasting time on tools that won't work for your company.

Define the rubric *before* the selection process begins. I find that defining (or redefining) the rubric afterwards results in endless rounds of conversations with too much focus on beating a specific vendor's capabilities (usually those of the first vendor you meet) in a small number of areas rather than looking at the bigger picture. Of course, this doesn't apply if you uncover previously unconsidered criteria. In these cases, revisit previously scored vendors quickly while memories are fresh.

Finalizing your rubric might get tricky when one or more stakeholders—who *initially* seemed super invested in the tool selection—go radio silent and don't share or approve their criteria. When that happens, here's the approach I usually take:

- **Set a fake deadline** - Give stakeholders about 1–2 weeks to submit their input, ensuring it's ahead of the actual deadline you've planned in your head.

- **Send plenty of reminders** - Use all your usual communication channels to remind them that if they miss the deadline, decisions will be made without their input to hit critical dates.

- **Fill in the blanks** - If the deadline comes and goes without their input, define their rubric dimensions for them and ask for approval by a date, letting them know that silence will be considered acceptance. (Sometimes, you have to have sharp elbows.)

- **Escalate strategically** - Share the rubric with senior leaders, which typically includes their bosses. This tends to grab attention and prompts them to weigh in.

- **Update and share:** Revise the rubric with any new feedback, then reshare it broadly, clearly highlighting the updates. It gives you a paper trail that demonstrates you did all you could to get everyone's feedback.

This (admittedly passive-aggressive) process not only keeps things moving but also ensures accountability without endless waiting.

Tackling the mid-year program launch challenge

Programs launched mid-year often face an uphill battle, struggling to gain traction during their first six months. This is usually how it plays out: buy-in is tough, people resist changing established workflows, and experimentation feels like a distraction from pressing priorities. This isn't unique to experimentation—it also happens with growth initiatives and other new programs. The problem isn't the program itself; it's the timing.

Mid-year, companies are typically scrambling to hit their existing goals, none of which account for your new experimentation program because it wasn't part of their original plans. As a result, your program gets sidelined, and building momentum feels nearly impossible. But there are actionable steps you can take to change this trajectory.

- **Secure bandwidth on the upcoming roadmap** - Your priority should be getting experimentation into the *next period's* plans (e.g. quarter or year). Meet with leaders, peers, and their managers to emphasize why experimentation is critical for achieving long-term goals. Verbal buy-in is a start, but persistence is key—don't stop until you see experimentation mentioned on official roadmaps and plans as part of product discovery, release cycles, etc. Start doing this when annual planning begins (or slightly before, ideally). The earlier you're included in these strategic discussions, the easier it will be to integrate experimentation into team workflows.

- **Make experimentation part of how features are shipped** - If you can partner with the head of product and/or engineering and make experimentation a part of the software development lifecycle (SLDC), then experimentation becomes the way things are done. You will probably have to work out the scenarios that don't require a test (e.g. critical bug fixes) and the tech stack to support that workflow (e.g. feature flagging), but if you can pull it off, you'll be in a great place.

- **Make experimentation part of decision-making -** Encourage decision-makers to request experiment results as part of any business case presented to them. While this shift may be challenging at first, it creates a trickle-down effect - teams will see experimentation as a natural part of how things are done. Over time, this helps embed a culture where decisions are grounded in data and experimentation is in everyone's toolbox.

- **Shape future talent and onboarding -** There isn't a great deal you can do about the co-workers you have, but you can influence the ones you will. Push to add language to job descriptions highlighting the importance of experimentation, ensuring new hires come in with the right mindset. Take it further by incorporating experimentation into onboarding programs. New employees are eager to prove themselves and can quickly become strong allies in driving a testing culture. By shaping how new hires approach their work, you're planting seeds for long-term program success.

Launching a program mid-year is no easy feat. But if you are strategic, persistent, and forward-thinking, it will pay off in the future.

Deciphering job postings

If you're reading this book, there is a non-zero probability that you are interested in landing a job leading an experimentation program. But before you start applying to every experimentation role you see, be mindful of some key terms and phrases that shed some light on the kind of environment in which the experimentation program operates. Here are some terms to watch out for to prepare some answers for interviews.

Terms/Phrases in the Job Description	What they say about the work environment
Self-starter	Your direct manager will not have a lot of time for you.
Fast-paced	Everyone and everything is understaffed.
Scrappy	You won't have much support - they really hope you solve things yourself.
Family	They have pizza parties and probably a ping-pong table. There is a high probability that they have a toxic culture.
Autonomous	No one really understands the space. They want someone's guidance.
Work with autonomous teams	You'll have to herd cats and strong personalities.
Hit the ground running	You won't have time to ramp up. Expect to deliver results a couple of weeks after starting.
Results-oriented	Your program better be ROI positive. You will have pressure placed on you.
Ability to present complex data clearly	Leadership doesn't understand statistics.

(Continued on the next page.)

(Continued from the previous page.)

Terms/Phrases in the Job Description	What they say about the work environment
High attention to detail	They are risk-averse.
Promote a data-driven approach	Most don't believe in A/B testing yet.
Work with Analytics teams	You won't have a dedicated statistician.
Manage multiple projects simultaneously	There are far too many OKRs, projects, and initiatives. They are understaffed.
Collaborative approach	There are siloes. Someone might yell at you if you aren't careful.

Advice from CRO experts

The DID prioritization framework

Eddie Aguilar

Co-founder of Ensure Financial

in /in/whoiseddie/

DID = Data, Ideas, Decisions; three key areas of experimentation that most typically bypass or think of retroactively.

*In the DID model, you consider the past **data** available, if the **idea** is feasible — does it require extra hands, complex code, shareholders involved, or integrations — and the **decisions** that need to be made from the results soon after an experiment ends.*

This prioritization model is based on whether all three key areas are defined and available, which means the experiment or hypothesis should be prioritized.

Finer points about prioritization

Shiva Manjunath

Senior Product Manager (CRO)

[in] */in/shiva-manjunath/*

While it would be amazing if we had unlimited resources and unlimited swimlanes to test everything all the time at once whenever we wanted, that reality exists for very few companies. Knowing that we have limited resources, we HAVE to make sure we run an efficient optimization program (Isn't that what we do? Why not optimize our testing process while we optimize sites?)

As best as you can, create questions in a scoring framework that are as objective as possible to help make scoring as consistent as possible. For example, if you have a question in your framework which asks, "Is the change above the fold?" – this can be rolled up to a 'reach' score in a RICE framework (if it's below the fold, it will have less visibility, which means less reach). Another example would be for confidence – every research method that backs a specific idea gives it a bonus bump in score (or, I guess technically a "penalty" for it not existing). You and I will answer these questions exactly the same way every time, and that makes scoring consistent and reliable.

Something else a prioritization framework helps with is DE-prioritizing ideas. If you have a test that will take a TON of Effort and has low Confidence (in a RICE framework, for example), compared to tests that have less effort and high confidence, that test will be deprioritized. Then, when that huge test someone keeps trying to run, which will take forever to build and has no data backed in it, you can just blame the framework. ;)

Enabling strategy with experimentation

Juliana Jackson

*Associate Director, Data & Digital Experience
EMEA at Monks*

in /in/juliana-jackson/

Experimentation is most impactful when it shifts from being a tactical exercise to a strategic enabler. While an OEC is a great way to measure broader impacts, the real power lies in how those metrics are chosen and communicated. Tracking ripple effects matters as long as we make sure they align with the company's bigger goals.

For example, if retention or customer lifetime value is a key focus for your business, experiments should be designed to reflect those priorities, not just in the outcomes they measure but in the questions they aim to answer. This approach transforms experimentation from a tool for optimization into a driver of strategic clarity.

A key insight I've learned is that success isn't just about running experiments but also about building trust and alignment across teams. When stakeholders from sales, marketing, engineering, and leadership collaborate on defining what success looks like, experiments stop being isolated activities and start becoming opportunities for shared wins. This requires breaking down silos and ensuring everyone feels invested in both the process and the outcomes.

Whether it's app development or experimentation, when teams work in isolation, you end up with disjointed results and missed opportunities. Experiments should not just deliver metrics, they should deliver clarity, alignment, and momentum. By designing experiments that answer strategic questions and reflect cross-functional priorities, you transform them into a tool that drives real business impact.

Navigating Engineering-led and Marketing-led companies

Juliana Amorim

Founder of Croct
🔗 */in/amorimj/*

In some contexts, you'll find that your company can be kind of engineering-led and marketing-led at the same time, which can be challenging. The secret lies in truly understanding what each one of these teams considers non-negotiable and what they're ready to compromise.

I would say the nonnegotiable criteria for engineers are the overall performance of the application and having the guarantee nobody will break the design system or the application itself, so they look for at least some kind of fault tolerance mechanism.

On the other hand, although non-technical people look for a no-code, intuitive interface, this doesn't necessarily mean having a visual editor. When you think about this, there is a good set of options for you to start from.

Communicating effectively for buy-in and collaboration

Kay del Rosario

Founder and Chief Strategist at Love Letter Emails

in /in/kaydelrosario/

Sharing progress during testing can be tricky, especially when you're dealing with company dynamics. Early on, I had moments where I felt like I had to put on a show, only sharing the good stuff and glossing over the not-so-good stuff. I learned that doesn't work. People see through it, and it just creates more pressure on you. Being honest and practical always works better, even if it means having some awkward conversations along the way. Here's what works for me:

Start with what to expect

- *Make it about learning, not winning. Never hype up tests like they are going to solve all your problems. That just sets everyone up for disappointment. Instead, I frame it like, "This test will help us understand what's working and what's not. It's a chance to get smarter about our users."*

- *Managing expectations helps everyone focus on learning, takes the pressure off you and your team, and keeps people from expecting huge, instant results.*

Speak to people in their language

- *For leadership, I stick to what they care about: the big-picture stuff. They don't need a play-by-play, just how the test ties into retention or revenue.*

- *Whenever you can, use numbers to keep things tangible: "We've seen a 15% higher click rate when we focus on benefits instead of features. This could mean more users stay engaged early on."*

- *For the team: Get into the details. They want to know how and why you're testing. Explain the hypothesis, what's working, and what's not working.*

- *Even if a test fails, always share the takeaways: "This didn't work, but it confirmed users don't respond to vague calls to action. That's useful for the next round."*

Don't ignore the politics

- *Testing can ruffle feathers, especially if it challenges someone's favourite idea. I've learned it helps to involve people early and acknowledge their input.*

- *For example: "The product team flagged a key user behaviour that helped us shape this test. Their insights made a big difference."*

- *Framing it as a group effort keeps things smooth and helps avoid anyone feeling sidelined.*

Use visuals to tell the story

- *Charts or screenshots go a long way. Data is important, but people connect more with something they can see.*

- *Once, I shared a screenshot of a user's reply to an email we tested. It made communicating the results better than any graph because it showed the real impact the test was having.*

Be real about setbacks

- *Not every test is going to knock it out of the park. Whatever the results, just own it: "This didn't hit the way we hoped, but it taught us what not to do, which is just as important."*

- *People respect honesty, it builds trust.*

At the end of the day, sharing progress isn't just about results, it's about how you communicate them. It's about showing you're learning and demonstrating that every test, win or lose, is part of a larger effort to improve. Clear and honest communication builds trust, keeps the team aligned, and helps everyone understand why the work matters. When your communication invites collaboration, you make others feel included in the process, which turns experiments into a shared journey. That's how you keep people invested and create the kind of momentum that drives meaningful progress.

Chapter 5 summary

- Challenges like misaligned stakeholders, shifting priorities, and conflicting goals can derail progress.

- Using prioritization frameworks (like ICE or RICE) helps focus efforts objectively, reducing unnecessary drama.

- Choosing an A/B testing platform is often political; align with budget owners and key teams to avoid roadblocks. Avoid building an in-house tool unless necessary—it's rarely worth the effort.

- Training and communication are key—keep statistics simple, tailor updates to your audience, and share progress transparently.

Chapter 6

TL;DR

If you've gotten to this part of the book, you are probably thinking of at least one of the following:

- This book is too long to read.
- This book took too long to read.
- This book is taking too long to read.
- It was a decent read, but I don't remember half of it, and I don't feel like re-reading it.
- I have a meeting in 5 minutes; just tell me what I need to know!

If this is the case for you, I've got you covered. Here are most of the key takeaways from this book—I hope they prove valuable in your work.

1. **The experimentation culture trifecta** - You need three things to have a healthy experimentation culture: Delivery, Insight, and Buy-in.

2. **Experimentation Isn't Just About Data, It's About Politics** - Your job isn't just about running tests; it's about convincing stakeholders that experimentation helps the business. If you can't

prove value, your program will be at risk.

3. **Use the GROW Framework to Keep Your Program Alive** - Seriously. I created an image that you can cut out of this book and keep with you. What more do you want? OK fine. I'll summarize it again here:

   o **Goals That Resonate** - Align your program's goals with what matters to stakeholders. They only care about what impacts them.

   o **Your Reputation Matters** – Being likable and building trust is just as important as being right. If people don't like working with you, they won't support your program.

   o **Optimize for Progress** – Keep showing momentum, even when test results aren't groundbreaking. Leadership needs to see continuous progress.

- Welcome Feedback – Stay adaptable and be prepared for pushback. Politics and internal resistance will always be factors.

4. **Stakeholder Management is Everything** – Understand who has decision-making power and what motivates them. Some leaders care about revenue, others about stability, and some just want to avoid looking bad. Speak their language. Leverage priority frameworks, dashboards and rubrics to your advantage.

5. **Build a Trophy Case** – Keep a repository of test wins and learnings ready at all times. Leadership will eventually ask for proof that your program is worth the investment—be prepared.

6. **Experimentation is a Marathon, Not a Sprint** – The initial excitement will fade. Wins will be harder to come by. Leadership priorities will shift. Your program survives by consistently proving its impact, keeping communication strong, and integrating experimentation into the company's DNA.

7. **Watch out for red flags** - Keep your eyes peeled and be prepared to act quickly if you want to save your program.

8. **Don't build your own A/B testing platform** - You can almost always invest those resources in something more impactful.

9. **Use the term *HiPPOcrites* often** - Feel free to use it in all your presentations, but if you do, tell people about this book! OK, this last point isn't *that* important. ;)

Chapter 7
Thank you

First off, thank you for taking the time to dive into this book and explore the ups and downs of navigating the politics of launching an A/B testing program. I hope it's given you not only some practical tips to work with but also the motivation to push through challenges and make real changes in your organization.

A huge shoutout to these amazing contributors who shared their expertise, stories, and insights to make this book what it is. I'm incredibly grateful for your generosity and your commitment to helping others thrive in this ever-evolving field. In no particular order:

Ana Catarina	Lucas Vos
Claire More	Nathan Pedrozo
Eddie Aguilar	Rosalie Suarez
Ellie Hughes	Sam Barber
Erin Weigel	Shannon Mulligan
Gintarė Forshaw	Shiva Manjunath
Ishan Goel	Tim Thijsse
Juliana Amorim	Ton Wesseling
Juliana Jackson	Tracy Laranjo
Kay del Rosario	Will Feng
Khalil Guliwala	

I founded **Experiment Nation** (ExperimentNation.com) to foster a global community of curious, data-driven practitioners like yourself. If you found this book helpful, consider the following:

- **Join Experiment Nation's newsletter** to receive insights, stories, and updates from experimenters worldwide.

- **Follow us on YouTube or TikTok,** where we share interviews, case studies, and actionable tips to keep you ahead of the curve.

- **Reach out.** Whether you have feedback, questions, or simply want to share your experiences. I would love to hear from you!

Keep experimenting, stay curious, and remember—you're not alone in this.

Warm regards,
Rommil

Chapter 8
Useful resources

With a little help from my friends

At the beginning of this book, I mentioned that this would not cover the totality of the field of experimentation. However, luckily for you, I, along with those who contributed to this book, have compiled a list of resources and conferences that are useful for experimentation practitioners of every skill level.

Newsletters

- Beyond the Mean by Juliana Jackson
  julianajackson.substack.com
- CRO weekly by Tom van den Berg
  tomvandenberg.substack.com
- Experimental Mind by Kevin Anderson
  kevinanderson.nl/newsletter
- Experiment Nation by Rommil Santiago
  experimentnation.com
- Growth Waves by Daphne Tideman
  growthwaves.beehiiv.com
- No Hacks by Slobodan Manic
  nohackspod.com
- Ruben de Boer's newsletter
  conversionideas.com/author/rubendeboer

Podcasts

- 1000 Experiments Podcast

  creators.spotify.com/pod/show/abtasty

- Customers Who Click

  customerswhoclick.com/customers-who-click-podcast

- Experimentation Masters

  firstprinciples.ventures/experimentation-masters-podcast

- Experiment Nation

  youtube.com/@experiment-nation

- From A to B by Shiva Manjunath

  creators.spotify.com/pod/show/from-a-to-b

- Growth Minded Superheroes Podcast

  open.spotify.com/show/2HF8p500AFxzoR4wxzP7V7

- Lenny's Podcast

  youtube.com/@LennysPodcast

- No Hacks

  nohackspod.com

- Standard Deviation

  juliana-jackson.com/standard-deviation-podcast

Academic reading

- Journal of Knowledge Management by the Operational Research Society

Books

- Design for Impact by Erin Weigel
- Don't Make Me Think by Steve Krug
- Experimentation Works by Stefan Thomke
- Freakanomics by Malcolm Gladwell
- Kill Your Conversion Killers by Joris Byron
- Making Websites Win by CRE
- Obviously Awesome by April Dunford
- Thinking, Fast and Slow by Daniel Kahneman

Websites

- AB Testguide calculators
  abtestguide.com
- Analytics Toolkit by Georgi Georgiev
  blog.analytics-toolkit.com
- Conversion Ideas by Ruben de Boer
  conversionideas.com/author/rubendeboer/
- CXL's training programs
  cxl.com/institute/programs/conversion-optimization

- Experimentation Culture Awards

  experimentationcultureawards.com
- Experiment Nation

  experimentnation.com
- Guess the Test by Deborah O'Malley

  guessthetest.com
- Koalatative

  koalatative.com
- Speero's List of AB testing tools

  speero.com/ab-testing-tools
- Steven Van Belleghem

  stevenvanbelleghem.com
- Thinking Bell by Ishan Goel

  thinkingbell.org

Conferences / Events

- Analytics Summit

  analytics-summit.com
- CODE@MIT

  ide.mit.edu/events/conference-on-digital-experimentation-code
- Conversion.Events

  Conversion.events
- Conversionboost

  conversionboost.dk
- ConversionJam

  conversionjam.com

- Conversion Talks

  conversiontalks.com
- Conversion Hotel

  conversionhotel.com
- EXL

  speero.com/exl
- Experimentation Culture Awards

  experimentationcultureawards.com
- Experimentation Elite

  experimentationelite.com
- Experimentation Island

  experimentationisland.com
- Growth Minded Superheroes

  growthmindedsuperheroes.com
- MeasureCamp

  measurecamp.org
- Superweek

  superweek.hu

Index

A

C

D

E

About the author

Over the last 15 years, I've built my career at the intersection of experimentation, growth, product management, marketing, and analytics. I've successfully navigated the complexities of launching and scaling experimentation programs, managing cross-functional teams, and fostering cultures of data-driven decision-making within challenging organizational environments.

Most recently, I served as Senior Director of Product Experimentation at leading email marketing company. Before that, I was the Director of Solution Strategy of Experimentation at one of the most popular A/B platform vendors. During my time at Canada's largest retailer, I worked as the Director of Growth Product, where I led experimentation, SEO, analytics platform, and product-led growth. Before that, I worked at various startups and international SaaS companies across over a dozen industries. You could say that I've been around the block a few times.

In 2019, I founded Experiment Nation (ExperimentNation.com) to give CROs and experimenters a platform to share their insights and amplify their voices. With thousands of followers worldwide, Experiment Nation reaches its audience through YouTube, its weekly newsletter, and virtual events.

Finally, in my spare time, I play way too much volleyball in the Toronto area, share my modest photography on Instagram (@rommil), and swear more often than I should — at least according to my long-suffering wife.

(Damn right I do.)

www.ingramcontent.com/pod-product-compliance
Lightning Source LLC
Chambersburg PA
CBHW071344210326
41597CB00015B/1553